D1165334

✷✷✷✷✷✷✷✷✷✷✷✷✷✷✷✷✷

BASEBALL
SUPERSTARS

Bernie Williams

✷✷✷✷✷✷✷✷✷✷✷✷✷✷✷✷✷

Hank Aaron

Ty Cobb

Lou Gehrig

Derek Jeter

Randy Johnson

Mike Piazza

Kirby Puckett

Jackie Robinson

Ichiro Suzuki

Bernie Williams

✶✶✶✶✶✶✶✶✶✶✶✶✶✶✶✶

BASEBALL
SUPERSTARS

Bernie
Williams

Clifford W. Mills

CHELSEA HOUSE
PUBLISHERS
An imprint of Infobase Publishing

✶✶✶✶✶✶✶✶✶✶✶✶✶✶✶✶

BERNIE WILLIAMS

Chelsea House
An imprint of Infobase Publishing
132 West 31st Street
New York NY 10001

Library of Congress Cataloging-in-Publication Data
Mills, Cliff, 1947-
  Bernie Williams / Clifford W. Mills.
      p. cm. — (Baseball superstars)
  Includes bibliographical references and index.
  ISBN-13: 978-0-7910-9468-6 (hardcover)
  ISBN-10: 0-7910-9468-5 (hardcover)
  1. Williams, Bernie. 2. Baseball players—United States—Biography. 3. New York Yankees (Baseball team) I. Title. II. Series.
  GV865.W55M55 2007
  796.357092—dc22
  [B]   2007005698

Series design by Erik Lindstrom
Cover design by Ben Peterson

Printed in the United States of America

Bang EJB 10 9 8 7 6 5 4 3 2 1

This book is printed on acid-free paper.

CONTENTS

A Cultural Ambassador for Baseball and the Country

The Treaty Room at the U.S. Department of State headquarters is a big, beautiful, and famous room. It is on the seventh floor of the Harry S. Truman Building, the third-largest federal building in Washington, D.C. The building's roof covers some seven acres. Ambassadors from all over the world meet in the Treaty Room and other reception rooms in the Truman Building to negotiate war, peace, and the future of the world.

On December 13, 2004, Secretary of State Colin Powell spoke to an important audience in the Treaty Room. The people gathered there were cultural ambassadors appointed to represent the United States in other countries. These ambassadors were leaders in their fields. One was Debbie Allen, an award-winning dancer and choreographer who had just returned

Colin Powell *(left)*, then the U.S. secretary of state, greeted New York Yankees center fielder Bernie Williams during a ceremony on December 13, 2004, to honor the efforts of the State Department's cultural ambassadors. Through the department's CultureConnect program, Williams traveled to South America in February 2005.

from China. Another was Yo-Yo Ma, a celebrated musician. Daniel Libeskind, a famous architect, was in attendance, as was Wynton Marsalis, an extraordinary jazz performer. Some were cultural ambassadors from other countries.

The newest ambassador in the cultural-exchange program, called CultureConnect, was a professional baseball player who also happened to be a gifted jazz guitarist. His name was Bernie Williams. He, too, was accomplished in his field, which happened to be center field for the New York Yankees. He was also a legend in his native Puerto Rico—so popular there that he was mobbed wherever he went. His popularity was about to grow in other countries, as well.

Colin Powell and Patricia Harrison, the assistant secretary of state for educational and cultural affairs, introduced Williams to the other ambassadors. Powell and Harrison were asking Williams to travel as a cultural ambassador to Venezuela and Colombia in February 2005. He listened intently as Powell addressed the audience:

> When it comes to helping people better understand America, the greatest ambassadors we have are the creators of American culture. We started the CultureConnect program two years ago to contribute unique American voices to the growing conversation within our globalized world. . . . You [the cultural ambassadors] are not only role models for the youth you meet around the world, you are an inspiration to your fellow Americans as well, who dream of building a better future.

THE AMBASSADOR IN VENEZUELA

When he began the five-day trip to Venezuela and Colombia, Williams knew that both countries had undergone political turmoil and had hunger and poverty rates much higher than those in the United States. He also knew that he would be in a certain amount of danger as a visible foreign celebrity. Williams was not afraid and was determined to look beyond politics and poverty to see the people. He wanted to have a positive influence on others and was not going to let any obstacle get in his way.

Williams met the U.S. ambassador to Venezuela, Bill Brownfield, in Caracas, the country's capital. He spent a few days there teaching baseball clinics and meeting with young people at parks and baseball fields. He even went to a concert. Williams was a hit with everyone he met. While Williams was doing an interview in the dugout of a ball field in Caracas, a 10-year-old boy climbed a high concrete wall, stuck his head through an opening, and handed his jersey to Williams to sign. Williams smiled broadly and invited the boy in. Five-year-olds began to wear sunglasses to pose as smaller versions of Williams. One boy, Jolmon Avedano, imitated his new hero by wearing black under his eyes and holding Williams's face close to his for all to compare. He wanted Williams to listen to him and to him alone. Most of the children felt that way.

Williams left Venezuela reluctantly, with a new appreciation of the country's young people and their challenges. He had ventured out of the sheltered world of a professional athlete and opened himself to others in a way that he seldom had before. He knew that Colombia was next on the itinerary, and his safe and secure world back in the United States would be very far away.

TRAVELING IN COLOMBIA

As soon as Williams arrived in Bogotá, Colombia, a military officer briefed him about security procedures. For decades, Colombia has endured a conflict involving rebel guerrilla groups, paramilitary militias, and drug trafficking. The officer told Williams that some 14,000 rebels were trying to overthrow the Colombian government, about 12,000 soldiers were

Bernie Williams offered tips to young players during a baseball clinic in Caracas, Venezuela. During his trip as a cultural ambassador in February 2005, he also visited three cities in Colombia. In that country, he was under constant guard to make sure he would not be kidnapped.

trying to stop them, and a great number of Colombians simply wanted to protect their drug business. He explained that Williams was in danger of being kidnapped and that he would be sticking close to Williams. "You could die here. My job is to make sure that doesn't happen," the officer said.

Williams listened carefully and then did something he often does when he is a little stressed. He took out his black guitar and began to strum. He closed his brown eyes and bobbed his head gently to the rhythm. Williams always finds comfort in sliding his long and graceful fingers across the six strings. He has used the guitar as a way to lose himself in a calmer world ever since he was eight years old, when he picked up his father's Spanish guitar and began to imitate his father's playing.

If Williams wondered at that moment whether this five-day trip to South America was worth the risks he was taking, he never let on. After the briefing, an officer with the U.S. Embassy, Gustav Goger, escorted Williams to a 9,000-pound

☆ ☆ ☆ ☆ ☆ ☆

CULTURAL EXCHANGE

After the terrorist attacks of September 11, 2001, the U.S. State Department began a number of programs to help Americans understand other cultures and to help people of other cultures understand us. One of those initiatives is CultureConnect, a program started in 2002 by Patricia Harrison, who was then the assistant secretary of state for educational and cultural affairs. Her idea was to appoint cultural ambassadors from the United States who were leaders in the fields of entertainment, the arts, business, and sports. They would visit other countries and talk about the importance of education, understanding, achievement, and hope. The U.S. State Department also receives cultural ambassadors from other countries.

CultureConnect has worked well. Mary Wilson, a member of the singing group The Supremes, went to Mozambique, Botswana, and Bangladesh and told young audiences about the importance of getting tested for HIV/AIDS. Author Frank McCourt met with students in Israel and Algeria, recounted the poverty of his youth in Ireland, and urged young people to tell the stories of their own lives. Musician Wynton Marsalis went to Mexico in May 2004 and reached out to some 800 young adults in workshops and performances. Choreographer and producer Debbie

(4,082-kilogram) armored vehicle that was waiting near the tarmac with its engine running. "If they shoot out the tires, we'll keep moving," Goger said. Another embassy official joked about how much New York Yankees owner George Steinbrenner would pay in ransom if Williams were kidnapped. Williams replied that Steinbrenner would probably say he should have signed another center fielder.

★ ★ ★ ★ ★ ☆

Allen taught dance to hundreds of young people in Beijing and Shanghai. Actor Ron Silver went to China on the anniversary of the 9/11 attacks, in 2002, and spoke to thousands of young adults. Several other artists, athletes, and business executives have also taken part in the program.

Former Secretary of State Colin Powell has told several stories about the lighter side of the world of diplomacy. When young adults from other cultures come to the United States, they are often surprised by matters great and small. One young girl from Asia was shocked that Americans put ice cubes in their tea. Another student could not believe that American students drank milk with pizza in schools. Several Brazilian students visiting Chicago realized to their horror that they did not have enough money to pay for their dinner. They expected harsh punishment. When the waitress talked to her manager and then said, "We're glad to have you in America . . . we'll cover the difference," the students were fully aware of how generous Americans could be.

For information on the Cultural Programs Division of the U.S. State Department, visit http://exchanges.state.gov/education/citizens/culture/.

Williams was an effective teacher at the many baseball clinics he held in Colombia. He was the first American baseball player to conduct clinics there in more than 50 years. At Once de Noviembre Stadium in Cartagena, young players listened intently as Williams told them to stride smoothly into a pitch. One boy asked exactly how far to stride. A foot? 18 inches? Williams answered every question patiently and with the confidence of someone who knows his subject. Williams had been one of professional baseball's most feared hitters for more than a decade. He was a careful student of all aspects of the game; now, he was a careful teacher.

The nearly 2,000 fans in Cartagena watched as he took batting practice. He felt rusty after so many months off from playing, but soon the rust fell away. He began to smash home run after home run over the 315-foot (96-meter) fence in right field. Young players scrambled into the stands to catch the balls. They fought one another for the prized souvenirs. Police officers in green uniforms had to hold hands to prevent the fans from mobbing the field. Everyone wanted to get closer to "Ber-nie."

MAKING MUSIC

The last part of the South American trip was a 90-minute drive from Cartagena to Barranquilla, along the Highway of the Sea. Farmers walking with their burros on the narrow shoulder of the road must have wondered about the armored convoy passing them. Williams was met by dancers and a band for a clinic he was giving at Tomas Arrieta Stadium in the heart of Barranquilla. The fans chanted his name, followed by three claps. To them, he was a rock star. He told the 90 boys and one girl in his clinic that the town reminded him of Vega Alta, his hometown in Puerto Rico. The kids roared their approval. The only girl in the clinic, Cristina Vega, said to a reporter, "I hate the Yankees, honestly, because I like the Braves. But Bernie? He's Bernie."

On the last day of his trip, he went to the Universidad del Norte to play some music with the Etnia Latin Jazz Band. For Williams, who is naturally shy, the concert may have made him more nervous than any other part of the trip. The students in the band could not afford sheet music, so they were unable to play songs from Williams's jazz album, *The Journey Within.* Somehow, though, they found songs that they all knew.

Williams began the concert with a guitar solo. Then, the students joined in one by one. It was musical magic. Each responded to the others' music. When a blackout hit the auditorium, no one seemed to notice except the military officer guarding Williams. The lights came back on, and the band played on as well. For their encore, all the members came out wearing blue New York Yankees caps.

After five 18-hour days, it was time to go home. Williams said goodbye to his new friends, and his protectors, and boarded Avianca Airlines Flight 38 after going through four security checkpoints. He began to reflect on what he had seen and done. Williams had touched many young lives in both countries. He had preached to hundreds of baseball-obsessed young children that the safest route out of poverty and toward success was through education. His life had been touched as well. He had made friends he would keep for the rest of his life, and he would say later that this trip changed his life in many ways. "As much as I was impacting them, it was even more for me," he said in a *New York Times* article. "It opened up the boundaries of the world I live in. The world I used to live in." Williams was exhausted and had a serious viral infection. He knew that spring training was only a few days away. As he covered himself in two maroon blankets, he fell into a much deserved deep sleep and headed back to his other world.

Growing Up in Puerto Rico

Bernie Williams was born Bernabé Williams Figueroa, Jr., on September 13, 1968, in San Juan, Puerto Rico. His father, Bernabé, Sr., had grown up in Puerto Rico during the Great Depression and had vowed to pull himself out of the poverty that surrounded him and his family. Bernabé, Sr., joined the U.S. Merchant Marine in search of a career with stability and security. Before long, he was traveling to ports all over the world. He was a strong and restless man who loved the sea. He was also a quiet and reserved man who loved music. He soon found another love.

In New York City, Mr. Williams met a young woman named Rufina. She was a teacher taking part in an exchange program from Puerto Rico. She was educated, intelligent, and firm in her beliefs. She also happened to be beautiful. New York

City was an exciting place for them to meet, and they shared common experiences like being in the city and growing up in Puerto Rico. They quickly became close and were attracted to each other's differences as well as similarities. They knew they belonged together, and they soon were married.

From the moment Bernie, Jr., was born, they were devoted to him. As the firstborn son, he could do little wrong. The family of three soon became a family of four when Hiram was born in 1969. Not long after, the Williamses realized that raising two active young boys in the Bronx, where they were living, would present challenges. The Bronx was a more dangerous place than it is now. Also, because Mr. Williams was gone on long trips so often, he felt he needed to make a change. He, Rufina, Bernie, Jr., and Hiram left for Puerto Rico.

Moving back to the island meant that the boys would be able to spend more time outside and less time inside watching television. Mrs. Williams made sure of it. She was a specialist in education, and she knew the effects of positive influences on children at an early age. She passionately believed that children must be encouraged to develop their bodies and their minds, not just one or the other. While she pursued her master's degree in higher education at the University of Puerto Rico in San Juan, she made sure that her boys spent plenty of time at the university pool and gymnasium. Bernie, Sr., was always there to supervise when she could not. The boys were never left alone. Mr. Williams had given up his career in the Merchant Marine to be closer to his family. He found work as a dispatcher and security guard in San Juan. He sacrificed his life at sea, but he gained precious time with his boys.

The family had moved to Vega Alta, a city west of San Juan, the capital of Puerto Rico. The city now has more than 37,000 residents and is known for its beautiful beach, Cerro Gordo, and the Vega Alta Forest, a natural wonderland. One of the focal points of the city is its Catholic church, Immaculada

Concepción, and during the first week of December each year, the city celebrates the feast of the Immaculate Conception. Vega Alta was a wonderful and vibrant place in which to grow up. It has aspects of both the city and the country, with roads that lead down to the blue-green Caribbean Sea.

THE SPANISH GUITAR

Mr. Williams sometimes found it difficult to sleep at night, a problem sailors on land have to adjust to. He would get up, go into the living room, and often pick up a guitar he had bought in Spain during one of his many trips. He would usually begin by strumming it softly, and he was always trying to teach himself new melodies. He loved recalling the *bolero* songs he had heard when he was growing up. Bernie, Jr., could sometimes hear his father playing; he would lie in the darkness of his bedroom wondering what his father was thinking and feeling. Bernie loved the sound of the music; it got into his mind and his body, and would not let go. The tones made him want to dance, to move to their beat. Sleep could wait.

One day when he was eight years old, Bernie picked up his father's guitar and began to pluck the strings to hear what kinds of sounds they could make. He wanted to be like his father and learn how to express himself through this instrument. He wanted to understand the music and make it sound the way he had heard it. He would later tell a reporter, "I remember just being attracted to the music. When I had the opportunity to pick up a guitar, it was like it was inside of me. It was a challenge to learn how to play it. I didn't want to stop." Bernie often took the guitar out to the balcony of his home and practiced without really knowing what he was doing. He never felt like singing. That would call too much attention to himself. He just liked to play the guitar. Like many young people, Bernie was afraid of being different from others and of being rejected. Music helped him calm those fears.

Bernabé and Rufina Williams wanted their sons to have a well-rounded education, with interests in academics, athletics, and the arts. At a young age, Bernie Williams and his brother, Hiram, were enrolled with a music tutor. Those lessons paid off. Years later, Bernie *(right)* and Hiram, playing the cello, practiced before a 2003 performance at the House of Blues in Chicago.

Mrs. Williams and her husband knew the importance of education and enrolled Bernie and Hiram with a musical tutor. Soon, Bernie could play a Puerto Rican folk song called "Verde Luz," a remarkable achievement for an eight-year-old. When he was in seventh grade, Bernie was accepted into the prestigious Escuela Libre de Musica (the Free School of Music), which only the musically gifted can attend. He now became serious about his musical education and learned how to read and play classical music as well as popular songs.

ACADEMICS, ATHLETICS, ARTS

Mrs. Williams called them the three A's: academics, athletics, and the arts. She wanted her sons to be well-rounded and skilled in all three A's. She did not want her children to be good in only one area. Instead, she encouraged them to try many different activities, both physical and intellectual. Both parents also insisted that their children follow the golden rule: always treat others as you would like to be treated. Because of their parents' focus on a well-rounded education, Bernie and Hiram were exposed to many types of people—outgoing jocks, shy nerds, sensitive artists. Often, these groups did not easily mingle. Bernie and Hiram, though, could move among these different crowds more easily than most people. They felt at home with many kinds of people. This sort of upbringing would be invaluable for a future professional athlete who finds himself spending months on end with some very strong and distinct personalities.

Since Mr. Williams now had more time with his sons, he took them places where they could run, throw, and play. Bernie seemed to be a born runner. He was growing faster than many other children his age, and his long legs helped him run quicker than almost everyone. He was graceful in all that he did, including throwing and hitting a baseball. His father encouraged him to join the Mickey Mantle Leagues; few people remember his early days in organized baseball the way they remember Derek Jeter's, but he was clearly good enough to excel almost as soon as he began to play. Before too long, several baseball scouts noticed him and deemed him to be a "follow," someone they felt they should continue to track.

Bernie's first success as an athlete, however, was as a track star. At 15, he set the Puerto Rican record for his age group in the 400-meter dash. He had a pure running form, keeping his head level and his arms knifing through the air. He also was superb at the long jump, with his long strides carrying him well out into the jumping pit. He won four gold medals at an international meet in San Juan, and some considered him to be a candidate to make Puerto Rico's track team for the 1988 Olympics.

Bernie also had a good deal of success academically. His grade-point average in high school was 3.8 (out of 4.0). Half of his high school day at the Free School of Music was devoted to English, math, and science. (English is required in all Puerto Rican schools from the first grade, so almost all Puerto Ricans are bilingual, speaking Spanish at home.) The afternoon was devoted to music, and students were asked to specialize in one instrument as soon as possible. Bernie thought about concentrating on the piano, but he realized he could not drop the instrument he loved and felt a part of: the guitar. When he thought about attending a conservatory after graduation and becoming a professional musician, his parents asked him to think more practically. Why not become a doctor or a lawyer or an engineer? His father had worked his way out of grinding poverty, and he worried that his son would starve as a musician. Why not pursue his interest in biology and become a doctor?

Bernie was lucky. He was talented enough academically to pursue any profession he wanted. He was talented enough to play with the musically gifted and become a professional guitar player and teacher. He was gifted enough athletically to represent Puerto Rico in track in the Olympics. He was good enough at baseball to become a "follow." He had worked hard at all three A's. For many years, he awoke at 5 A.M. to get ready for school and did not return home until after 8:30 P.M. His hard work gave him many choices for a career, and he was about to choose one path over all the others.

BECOMING A YANKEE

The Free School of Music had no baseball team, so Williams had to join competitive leagues if he wanted to pursue baseball. The sport had two attractions for him. Williams, like many other Puerto Ricans, had an idol: Roberto Clemente, one of the first and best Latin players ever to compete in the major leagues. Clemente had played his career with the Pittsburgh Pirates before he was killed in a plane crash in December 1972, and he has been a legendary figure to Puerto Ricans ever since.

Bernie had another tie to baseball: His uncle Jedan Figueroa had been drafted by the Pittsburgh Pirates and had played briefly for Pittsburgh's minor-league team in Batavia, New York. Jedan was somewhat bitter about his experience; he had not been able to eat at the same restaurants as his teammates

☆ ☆ ☆ ☆ ☆

ROBERTO CLEMENTE

Game 6 of the 1971 World Series was a thriller. The powerful Baltimore Orioles were poised to win the game. Their star hitter, Frank Robinson, connected on a long fly ball to the Pittsburgh Pirates' right fielder, Roberto Clemente. On third base, Oriole Merv Rettenmund was ready to tag up and score. Clemente settled under the ball and prepared for the throw to home plate. Those who saw the catch and throw say it was one of the most amazing in baseball and World Series history. The ball hit Clemente's glove and was out and on the way home in a split second. Some say that everyone in the stadium could hear the ball whistling as it shot toward the Pirates catcher. If the ball had been pitched from the mound, it would have been called a strike. Rettenmund gave up halfway toward home, seeing that he was doomed if he kept running. The Pirates went on to win the World Series. One announcer said that Clemente could field a ball in New York and throw out a runner in Pennsylvania.

Clemente was born in Carolina, Puerto Rico, on August 18, 1934. He played 18 seasons with the Pittsburgh Pirates, from 1955 to 1972. He was a four-time National League batting champion, had a career batting average of .317, and finished because racial discrimination in the 1950s was everywhere, even in small-town upstate New York.

Bernie may not have played much baseball compared with other future stars, but his speed and general athletic ability made him a good baseball prospect. When he was 16 years old, the Pirates asked him to try out for their team. Williams went to their tryout camp in Dorado, Puerto Rico, on a particularly hot day. He ran the 60-yard dash (in which he presumably did very well), chased fly balls, threw to each base from the outfield,

☆ ☆ ☆ ☆ ☆

his career with exactly 3,000 hits, the eleventh player to reach that many. He won 12 Gold Glove awards (the most ever for an outfielder, a record shared with Willie Mays). He is one of only four players in major-league history to have more than 10 Gold Glove awards and a career batting average above .300. He was the second Hispanic player voted into the Baseball Hall of Fame (Lefty Gomez was the first, in 1972). What Jackie Robinson did for African-American players in opening up professional baseball, Clemente did for Latin players.

In late December 1972, a devastating earthquake hit the Central American country of Nicaragua. Clemente always spent much of his time during the off-season involved in charity work, and on New Year's Eve he coordinated the loading of a private plane with supplies for the earthquake relief effort. The plane crashed off the coast of Isla Verde, Puerto Rico, and Clemente's body was never recovered. One of his best-known fans, Bernie Williams, has said of Clemente: "Growing up in Puerto Rico, we got to learn a lot about his character; it was obvious that not only was he one of the greatest players, but a great human being as well."

Roberto Clemente, who played for the Pittsburgh Pirates from 1955 to 1972, is a hero in his native Puerto Rico. He won the National League batting title four times. Clemente died in a plane crash on December 31, 1972, when he was traveling to Nicaragua to deliver aid to earthquake victims there.

and took batting practice. The Pirates immediately offered him a contract. The team sent representatives to talk to the Williams family, and Uncle Jedan was waiting for them, with Rufina and Bernie, Sr. They all had questions, but Jedan especially knew the difficult questions to ask. He was determined to protect his 16-year-old nephew from some of the experiences he had gone through years earlier. The meeting did not go well, and no agreement was signed.

Meanwhile, a New York Yankees scout for Puerto Rico, Roberto Rivera, found out that Bernie had been to the Pirates camp. He had followed Bernie for years. He knew, though, that Bernie had been offered a track scholarship to the University of California, Los Angeles, and assumed that the offer was a first priority for the family. Rivera thought that baseball would lose in the fight for Bernie's attention, but he was now encouraged. He knew that Bernie was fast enough to cover all of center field, even in famously large Yankee Stadium, where the gaps in left-center and right-center field are large enough to drive herds of cattle through. He arranged to have Bernie flown to a Yankees tryout camp in Connecticut.

The Yankees were impressed with what they saw. They were so impressed that they would not let Bernie venture away from the camp for days, fearing that other teams would hear about this new prospect. They offered a contract worth $16,000 (more than the Pirates had offered). As soon as his seventeenth birthday came, on September 13, 1985, he signed his Yankee contract. Uncle Jedan was not needed this time. The contract signing was not the high-profile event that the Derek Jeter signing would be a few years later, when $800,000 changed hands after a long and complicated negotiation. The Yankees did not know it for another decade, but they had just signed an equally important player for a dynasty they would build in the last half of the 1990s. Bernie Williams was on his way to stardom, but the journey there would be a long and difficult trek.

The Climb Upward: 1985–1991

Bernie Williams signed his Yankees contract too late in the year to be able to jump right into professional baseball games at the minor-league level. So, he still had some time to consider a few more career options. His desire (and his family's desire for him) to become a doctor seemed to be getting stronger, yet the pull of music was always tugging at him. He had been taught that he could and should have many interests, and he never felt he had to choose between being a baseball player and a doctor. There would be time for both. Bernie felt he must try to get a college degree to expand his career options beyond baseball. He began classes at the University of Puerto Rico in San Juan. Still, baseball was a lure, and he was looking forward to his first professional baseball experience. He was going to leave his home for the first time and venture into a larger and more difficult world.

REPORTING TO FLORIDA

In the spring of 1986, Bernie reported to the Yankees' farm system and the Gulf Coast Rookie League in Fort Lauderdale, Florida. He was tall and thin—at 17 years old, he was 6-foot-2 and 160 pounds (188 centimeters and 72.5 kilograms). He was very fast and had remarkable natural reflexes. The Yankee coaches could see right away that he had plenty of natural ability but that he had much less baseball-playing time than most other minor-league prospects his age. He had not played nearly as many innings in game conditions as they had, and the coaches realized that Bernie needed some strong guidance. He was also still growing and not quite strong enough to be a home-run hitter. The Yankees did not have much need for a fleet-footed defensive center fielder who could only hit singles and doubles. They had major-league stars Dave Winfield and Rickey Henderson and several others who were strong hitters and played well on defense. In fact, the Yankees already had several good center fielders in their minor-league system, including two players who everyone thought would soon be stars: Roberto Kelly and Jay Buhner.

Bernie began to wrestle with an issue that he would soon resolve: How could he set himself apart from his competition within the Yankees? He had not been drafted among the top 10 prospects out of high school and he did not have much of a name within the organization. He was not from the American mainland and did not have a network of coaches and reporters asking about his progress and keeping him visible within the very large and sprawling Yankee organization. Getting noticed in the minor leagues is no different from getting noticed at any other desirable job with considerable competition, and Williams needed to find an edge. He would soon.

The first few months of adjusting to the life of a minor-league professional baseball player can be difficult. At first, Derek Jeter used to call home every day for emotional support from family and friends. Bernie Williams was only 17 and not able to accompany his minor-league teammates to bars and nightclubs. Instead, he stayed in his hotel room and found some comfort in music—the one diversion that had always made him relaxed and taken him away from his problems and everyday cares. He listened to and soaked up the blues, jazz, popular music, Latin beats, and classical music. He listened to CDs for hours on end. He did not need any other outlet during his time away from the baseball field.

When his first minor-league season came to an end, Williams headed home to Vega Alta. His first year was unremarkable—he batted .270 with 2 home runs and 25 RBIs in 61 games. Everyone knew that he had potential, but some felt that his many interests showed a lack of drive toward one ambition: major-league success. An intense focus is always stressed in professional sports, and Williams had trouble narrowing his many interests. He was as much an artist as an athlete, and he was still young enough not to want to choose one side of himself over another.

FINDING THE EDGE

During minor-league spring training in 1987, Williams decided to try something that would make him stand out. He experimented with becoming a switch-hitter—someone who bats from either side of home plate. A switch-hitter is rare in baseball, because training the mind and eyes to react to two different pitching angles is a difficult task. A true switch-hitter, someone who is equally good from both sides of the

Batting left-handed, Bernie Williams struck a two-run home run against the Atlanta Braves in the 1996 World Series. As a young minor leaguer, Williams was looking for a way to distinguish himself from all the other quality center fielders in the Yankee organization. Williams, who was a natural right-handed batter, decided to become a switch-hitter.

plate, is even rarer. Williams vowed to make himself a true switch-hitter. He was a natural hitter from the right-hand side, and he realized that it would take years to feel as natural hitting from the left. During 1987, he played 25 games for Fort Lauderdale in the Florida State League and 25 games for Oneonta in the New York–Penn League. A shoulder injury in

☆ ☆ ☆ ☆ ☆

THE BASEBALL

A baseball is a surprisingly complicated piece of work. It has a cork-rubber composite nucleus, which is completely enclosed in rubber. That core is wrapped in 121 yards (111 meters) of blue-gray wool yarn, 45 yards (41 meters) of white wool yarn, and 120 yards (110 meters) of cotton yarn. All of this is covered with two pieces of cowhide (replacing the horsehide used in the early days of the game). The pieces of the cover are hand-stitched together with raised red cotton stitches. The stitches help the ball cut through the air; if the ball were smooth, it would travel about 15 percent less in distance than it does with stitches.

For many years, professional-league baseballs were made in Chicopee, Massachusetts, but when labor costs became too expensive, they started to be made in Haiti and then Taiwan. In 1990, major-league balls began to be produced solely in Costa Rica. The manufacturers have strict standards; they are inspected by representatives from Major League Baseball. Yet, there is some leeway. The ball can be as heavy as 5¼ ounces and as light as 5 ounces (142 grams). Its circumference (measured at its "equator") can be as small as 9 inches (23 centimeters) or as large as 9¼ inches. Since temperature and humidity affect its size and weight, the ball is kept in a special humidor for at least two hours before the game. If a ball is frozen, it will lose

May interrupted his season at Fort Lauderdale, but when he returned to play at Oneonta, he batted .344.

The following season, Williams was sent to play for the Prince William Cannons in the Carolina League, a "high-A" team that is only a step below the tougher Double-A and Triple-A minor-league teams. The movie *Bull Durham* was

☆ ☆ ☆ ☆ ☆

about 25 feet (7.6 meters) off a 375-foot (114-meter) fly. If it is heated to 150°F (65.5°C), it will fly 25 feet farther on the same hit.

Before every professional baseball game, an umpire or locker-room attendant rubs down the baseballs (usually six dozen per game) with "Lena Blackburne Baseball Rubbing Mud." Blackburne was an infielder for many teams and was briefly the manager of the Chicago White Sox in the late 1920s (he was most known for fighting with his own players). He discovered a distinctive kind of mud and put it to use. The mud removes the slick and shiny outer coating from the cowhide, allowing pitchers to get a better grip for more control. Some have argued that this practice should be stopped, since it favors pitchers over hitters. The ball becomes slightly discolored and harder to see.

The mud is not just any mud. It is very fine, like a thick chocolate pudding. It comes from the Delaware River, near where George Washington crossed on Christmas night in 1776, prior to the Battle of Trenton, one of the most notable moments in American history. The actual location of the mud source is secret, like the formula for Coca-Cola. Some 900 pounds (408 kilograms) of it are dug up every July, canned, and sent all over the world, wherever baseball is played.

Hundreds of workers stitch covers onto baseballs at the Rawlings factory in Turrialba, Costa Rica. All of the baseballs used in the major leagues are produced at the facility in Costa Rica. The balls are manufactured under strict standards.

a fictionalized account of a real Carolina League team, the Durham (North Carolina) Bulls. Neither the Cannons nor the Bulls are still part of the league, but they were very much a part of it in 1988, when the movie appeared. The movie accurately portrayed the life of a minor leaguer, with the countless distractions, poor playing conditions, fast food, and low pay. Players, though, had to start somewhere. Barry Bonds played for Prince William in 1985, and several other future major leaguers were to come from the team. Fortunately for Williams, the hitting and fielding coaches at Prince William were thorough and patient.

Williams was also helped during this time—a crucial one in any baseball career—by the beginning of a change in the Yankees' philosophy: The Yankees were no longer trading away their best young prospects for experienced and expensive veterans, as they had for many years. The old philosophy had not produced any world champions, so a new strategy was needed. The organization was starting to wait for prospects to grow physically and emotionally, and develop more skills with more practice. In 1990, after Yankees owner George Steinbrenner was banned from baseball for paying a private investigator to get damaging information on one of his players, the team became even more focused on this strategy of developing its young players. (Steinbrenner was reinstated three years later.)

With the quality coaching at Prince William, Williams developed his switch-hitting and became better in the field, learning to anticipate when a line drive to center would come down to glove level. He still needed more awareness of where he was in the outfield, however; on July 14, 1988, he ran into an outfield wall chasing a fly ball and broke his wrist (minor-league fields often do not have the wall padding that major-league fields do). He had not tamed his own speed and was not always under control. Yet, he hit .335 for Prince William in 1988, the best batting average in the Carolina League. He also had 7 home runs and 45 runs batted in, both personal bests. Williams was starting to get power. He had gained 20 pounds (9 kilograms) of muscle from ages 17 to 20, and he was now looking like a major leaguer. His growth spurt ended, and his extraordinary physical coordination became even more obvious. His speed had always been a part of his game; he stole 29 bases for the Cannons, a team high. In November 1988, the Yankees put Williams on their 40-man roster, meaning no other team could try to sign him. They wanted to protect this budding "natural."

By the spring of 1989, Williams, and especially his switch-hitting, had made an impression on the Yankees' minor-league coaches. Sports reporter Michael Martinez filed this report from Fort Lauderdale for the *New York Times* on February 26, 1989:

> He is their phenom this spring, their kid with unlimited talent and untapped potential. He is only 20 years old, but the coaches who work with him daily say he has the skills of a big leaguer. The people in the front office speak of his intellectual and physical growth. They all say he simply can't miss. When he hears these things, Bernie Williams smiles and shrugs and says he hopes they are right. His youth prevents him from gloating immodestly.

The writer did not know Williams well and did not realize that his modesty came from his very nature, not his age. In the article, Frank Howard, the Yankees hitting coach in 1989, noted that Williams has "fantastic bat speed . . . and he has great reflexes." Bat speed and reflexes are skills that are not easily taught. Williams was finally being noticed, and he must have thought he was poised for his first major-league experience.

SLOWED PROGRESS

Williams had a solid spring training in 1989, but the Yankees wanted him to go back to the minors for another year of growth. Williams was disappointed, especially after all the good press he was getting, but he willingly headed off to the Yankee minor-league team, the Columbus Clippers. This Triple-A team had had many Yankees stars, and more would be on the way. Within the next five years, players named Derek Jeter and Mariano Rivera would join the Clippers. Williams, however, did not do as well as he wanted to there, struggling for 50 games. He was soon sent down to the Yankees' Double-A team in Albany, New York, a rapid and stinging demotion.

Some coaches thought that Williams was not applying himself fully. He was in his second year of courses at the University of Puerto Rico, studying biology and other subjects, and he was often studying into the night. He was very serious about getting his college degree, but he began to feel that he had to make a choice between baseball and education. It was a choice he had not wanted to make. In a similar vein, many felt that Williams's personality—shy and introverted—made him appear as if he did not have enough team spirit. Too often in sports, the loudest and brashest get noticed, rather than the best. Something was holding him back, but that would eventually change.

ALBANY DAYS AND NIGHTS

When Williams arrived in Albany, New York, in 1989 to play for the Double-A Albany-Colonie Yankees, he first looked for a place to stay. Some minor leaguers live with local families in exchange for errands or yard work, and others share a living space with teammates. Williams soon found an apartment near Hudson Valley Community College with two teammates, Ricky Torres and Oscar Azócar. He remembered the time fondly when he spoke to reporters later:

> Ricky did the cooking. I helped out, eating and doing the dishes once in awhile. He was a great cook. He cooked Latin food mostly, rice and beans, shrimp, seafood. We would barbecue after the games, too, sometimes at 11 or 12 at night. I had a great time. We didn't go out to clubs. I wasn't 21 yet. We did go to the movies. Ricky bought a little car—a very little car—that we used to get around.

Williams explored the area with his friends and tried scuba diving for the first time, in Lake George. Scuba diving had been for tourists in Puerto Rico, but Williams enjoyed how much he could see in a large lake. Growing up near the ocean in Puerto Rico, he took the water for granted. Now, he seized the chance to swim.

He enjoyed his bachelor life, but he would soon make a life-changing decision. Two years before, Williams met a wonderful young woman named Waleska while taking first-year biology at the University of Puerto Rico. She was intelligent and beautiful. He may have felt that his bachelor days were fun, but he could see how a deeper companionship would make him happier over the long run. On February 23, 1990, he and Waleska married in Puerto Rico and moved to the village of Colonie to begin the 1990 season with the Albany-Colonie Yankees.

Waleska and Bernie Williams loved the Albany area, and she feels that playing there was the turning point in his career: "Albany showed Bernie what type of player he can be. The contact with the fans—telling him they were counting on him and that he had ability—really gave him confidence." Waleska perhaps is being modest about the crucial role she played in giving Williams the drive and confidence to overcome his shyness. At the beginning of the 1990 season, he admitted, he was ready to quit baseball. He had been playing in the minor leagues for several years, and he had been so close to making it to the majors that he was simply frustrated. Minor leaguers can have long careers without ever going up to the big leagues, even for a cup of coffee (as a brief major-league stint is known), and the years of perpetual disappointment take their toll.

Most people close to the couple believe it is no accident that, after marrying Waleska, Bernie had more confidence in himself. Those close to Williams also know that his mother, Rufina, would have told him that he could not quit now. He had too much time invested. Soon, he also had a child to help him focus on his baseball career. Bernie Alexander was born in late 1990. Williams now had a family to support.

The final factor in his turnaround at Albany was coach Buck Showalter, who would be the New York Yankees manager from 1992 to 1995. Showalter knew that Williams had the potential to make it big, and he convinced Williams that his time was coming. He showed Williams that baseball is a combination of relaxation and concentration—being relaxed was not enough, nor was just concentration. Both were needed. Having

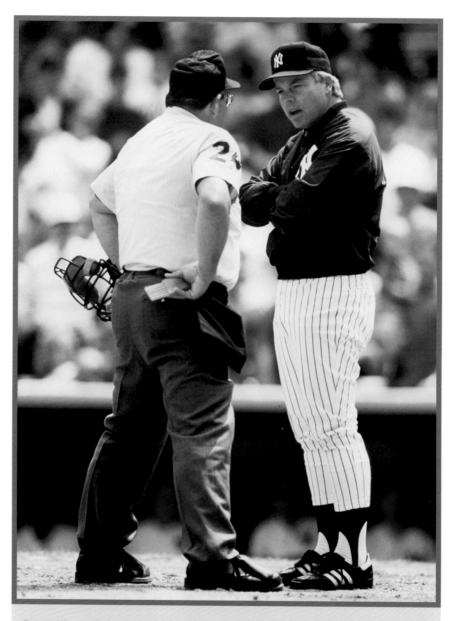

Buck Showalter, then the manager of the New York Yankees, argued with the umpire about a call during a May 1992 game against the Oakland Athletics. Showalter was the coach of the Yankees' Double-A farm team in Albany, New York, when Bernie Williams played there. Showalter helped Williams to build his confidence and develop as a player.

the right coach at the right time can be crucial to a young player, and Showalter was the right coach to build Williams's confidence. He knew that Williams was more sensitive than most players and did not need a coach who constantly shouted at him. Showalter gently pushed as well as openly encouraged Williams, and they began to trust each other. It was a relationship that would protect Williams later and would be one that Williams would never forget.

During the 1990 season at Albany, Williams batted .281 with 8 home runs and 54 RBIs. The next season, he moved back up to the Columbus Clippers. Through 78 games, against more quality players, he improved to a .294 batting average, with 8 home runs and 37 RBIs. And then he got his chance to move up.

MAJOR-LEAGUE DEBUT

Players never forget "The Call." The first time they hear a coach or a team executive say they must immediately report to their major-league team's park, the words become a part of their lives. Williams got "The Call" on July 6, 1991. Yankees center fielder Roberto Kelly, a young star in the making, sprained his right wrist when he ran into a wall while chasing a double by Cal Ripken, Jr. Kelly was put on the 15-day disabled list, and an unknown Yankees executive called Williams to tell him he needed to get to New York to join the Yankees.

Williams flew to New York, excited about his first chance to play in the major leagues, a dream he had had since he was old enough to throw a ball. One first impression he had was the difference between the clean, carpeted, and air-conditioned clubhouse at Yankee Stadium and the minor-league clubhouses he had been used to, with lockers rusted from sweat and beer and dirty floors covered with bugs of all sizes and shapes. There was no comparison. Williams felt that he had made it, at long last.

Yankees manager Stump Merrill put Williams in the lineup on July 7 against the Baltimore Orioles. Merrill was familiar with Williams, having seen him a number of times in minor-league games, and he had no second thoughts about starting him immediately. Williams told a reporter, "I've been dreaming of this since I signed, six years ago." From the dugout, he looked out at a crowd of 43,505. He later said, "I didn't expect this many fans." He was nervous, as most people would be under the circumstances. With the Yankees trailing, 3-0, Williams came to the plate in the fifth inning with the bases loaded. He was batting right-handed and hit a long fly to left field, just short of the wall in Yankee Stadium. The ball was caught, but the runner on third scored easily, and Williams had his first major-league run batted in and his first sacrifice fly. He was thrilled.

Many in the crowd were astonished when Williams caught up to a sinking liner off the bat of Chris Hoiles in the eighth inning. He dived for the ball, miraculously caught it, but then saw it fall out of his glove when he hit the ground hard. After the game, he told reporters, "I should have had it." Some reporters laughed, knowing that very few Yankee center fielders would have even come close.

BEING BULLIED

Baseball teammates constantly tease each other, usually in a good-natured way. Yankee Derek Jeter, who has an unusually large following of young female fans, had to put up with teammates cooing at him in their best impression of a 14-year-old girl asking him where he was going that night. Probably because Williams was an introspective and quiet man who liked to play the guitar near his locker after a game, he became the target of a significant amount of teasing during his early years with the Yankees. He soon had the nickname "Bambi." Some think that the name captured his shy and even

Bernie Williams ran the bases during a Yankees game on July 21, 1991, at Oakland. He had been called up to the majors just two weeks earlier after center fielder Roberto Kelly sprained his wrist.

bashful way of looking at others. Others believe his quick and graceful pursuit of fly balls in center field made him look like a deer running. Because Williams often wore glasses, he was teased about that, too.

In one case, the teasing turned darker and more hurtful. In 1989, the Yankees signed an outfielder named Mel Hall, who had a wonderful rookie year with the Chicago Cubs in 1983. After a car accident outside a hotel in Texas, however, he seemed to become injury-prone and unable to live up to his early promise. Once he joined the Yankees, he hoped to stay with them. Hall, who was flamboyant and loud, lived in the Trump Tower in Manhattan and had two pet cougars that he took for walks as often as he could. The city of New York had to confiscate the cougars and fined him $10,000.

From the moment they met, Hall seemed to enjoy needling Williams. He made fun of the guitar playing and of Williams's tendency to withdraw into himself and his music or studying after a game. The teasing soon turned into berating. Williams had been brought up not to respond to people who might want to intimidate him, and he did his best to avoid a confrontation. Buster Olney, a reporter who covered the Yankees for the *New York Times,* described Williams's nature:

> Angry words launch themselves from deep inside Bernie Williams, his emotional silos opening and unleashing responses aimed at hurting an antagonist, the way Williams hurts when someone else fires slashing words at him. He never fires the first shot—his parents weaned him of this instinct long ago, constantly reminding him that he needed to be respectful of others. Williams wants to retaliate, but before angry words escape his mouth, they lodge in his throat. They are choked off. He says . . . nothing. Williams tries to say something vicious, needs to say something nasty. Instead, he will stare softly and pause for five seconds or maybe 10, and sometimes, in his velvet

voice, he will spit out his best retort: "I can't believe you said that, man."

Psychologists think that one cause of bullying and aggression is frustration. When someone is blocked from reaching a goal, they can become aggressive. Hall's goal, no doubt, was to be a leading Yankee outfielder, and he may have felt that Williams would get in his way. Team veterans, like captain Don Mattingly, stood up for the shy rookie; Williams would never forget the kindness Mattingly showed him. Luckily for Williams, the Yankees and Hall decided to part company after the 1992 season. He has become a symbol of Yankee teams that had plenty of personalities but could not win championships.

Baseball teams have a real mixture of people and personality types, but the loud and flamboyant Yankees of the late 1980s and early 1990s were soon to change. In 1994 and 1995, the Yankees' Triple-A team in Columbus would include Derek Jeter, Mariano Rivera, Andy Pettitte, and Jorge Posada. These were players who were physically gifted and mentally prepared for ultimate success and its pressures. They had grown up in the Yankee organization. They always learned, and they always improved. The loud and losing Yankees were about to become their opposite. Williams had paved the way for a new group of Yankees to take over.

Rebuilding the Yankees: 1992–1996

The trip to the majors in 1991 was not to last. In more than 300 at-bats, Williams hit .238, not enough to keep him in the big leagues. He had a terrible day on August 21, striking out five consecutive times in a 7-4 loss to the Kansas City Royals, tying a major-league record. (One of the other players to hold this unfortunate record was the Yankees' hitting coach, Frank Howard.) Williams was sent back to the Triple-A Columbus Clippers for the 1992 season. Even though this was expected, the move hurt. For the second time, Williams questioned whether it was time to leave baseball. His character and his upbringing, though, saved him again. He would not quit. He would never quit. Also, he now had a taste of the Big Show, and he wanted more. Williams had not been very successful, but he now knew what he faced. He knew what he had to work on, including becoming a better hitter from the right side of the plate, where his batting average was lower than from the left side.

THE COLUMBUS CLIPPERS: 1992

One of the lessons Williams learned was that, no matter where a player found himself, he could listen to good coaching from many sources and decide what to use to make his game better. He need not become frustrated. Or, if he did, he could use that frustration to drive him. As Williams settled back to the Columbus Clippers in 1992, he realized he was lucky in many ways. He was surrounded by serious players who were collectively on the brink of storming the gates of major-league baseball. Manager Rick Down was demanding but fair, and a good teacher as well, especially in hitting. Like Showalter, he knew Williams would respond.

One of Williams's teammates in Columbus was J.T. Snow. Another was Brad Ausmus. Both would become stars for many years in the majors. Pitchers Bob Wickman and Scott Kamieniecki were outstanding for the team, and both would have successful careers as well. Eight Clippers made the minor-league All-Star team. Williams worked more on his hitting, and his average improved to .306. He began to get more clutch hits, helping to win games for the Clippers. The team had a record of 95 wins and 49 losses. The 1992 Clippers have been called one of the best minor-league teams of all time.

Winning at any level seems to feed on itself, as does losing. The success of the Clippers in 1992 helped Williams to get another chance at the big leagues. He was called up on July 31, 1992, when Danny Tartabull was placed on the disabled list. Williams became the only major leaguer to play in every inning of his team's games during the last two months of the season. In the majors in 1992, he ended up batting .280 in 261 at-bats, an improvement over the previous year's showing.

During the Yankees' 1993 spring training in Fort Lauderdale, Williams was better than ever. The combination of being with such a successful minor-league team and his success in the majors in 1992 helped sustain his confidence. Still, he was nearing 25, an unofficial cut-off point when minor leaguers begin to feel they will never make the majors. So he must have had doubts. "This is the time when I can't relax," he told a *New York Times* reporter during spring training. "It's nice to know they're counting on me, but you can't rely on that. You have to be able to perform well, especially here, if you want any security."

A PERMANENT CENTER FIELDER: 1993–1994

Center field is one of the most demanding positions in baseball. The center fielder is the quarterback of the outfield, calling out who has responsibility to cover what territory and make which catch. Center fielders must obviously be fast, since they cover some 50 percent of the outfield. They must have a good throwing arm, and they are expected to hit with power as well. The Yankees have a long tradition of brilliant center fielders, starting with Earle Combs in the 1920s and continuing with Joe DiMaggio and Mickey Mantle. Since Mantle's retirement in 1968, no one had been able to live up to the standard. That was about to change.

In 1993, Williams was called on—this time for good. His Yankees manager was his old mentor from Albany, Buck Showalter, who had replaced Stump Merrill in 1992. Williams did not have to prove himself to Showalter, and he began to flourish.

Williams established himself as a fielder who could get to any line drive and fly ball that stayed in the park. He even caught a few that left the park, reaching over fences to snag potential home runs. In 1993, he played in almost every game, and hit a respectable .268 for the year. He hit 12 home runs and drove in 68 runs, making him a productive if not especially powerful hitter. Williams also struck out 106 times, however, and many in the Yankees organization still wondered if he would be their permanent center fielder.

In 1994, Williams continued to improve, and he tightened his grip on the center-field job. His second child, Beatriz Noemi, was born on April 4, so he had even more family responsibilities. Williams applied himself more than ever, trying to improve his

★ ★ ★ ★ ★ ★

GEORGE STEINBRENNER

When George Steinbrenner and his partners bought the New York Yankees in 1973 for $8.7 million, most people at the time thought they had overpaid. In 2006, *Forbes* magazine estimated that the team was worth $1 billion. The Yankees have turned out to be a very good investment for Steinbrenner. At his first owners' meeting, he assured some of the most famous names in baseball ownership (including Gene Autry, Philip Wrigley, Tom Yawkey, Charlie Finley, Calvin Griffith, and Walter O'Malley) that he was in the shipping business and had no time to run the Yankees on a daily basis. He would be an uninvolved absentee owner. Those words turned out to be untrue. He has been one of the most influential, demanding, and notorious owners in sports history, both hated and loved.

Steinbrenner was born and grew up in the suburbs of Cleveland, Ohio. After two years in the U.S. Air Force, he coached high school basketball and football. Soon he joined his father's firm, the American Shipbuilding Company, and was so successful that he eventually bought it. In the 1970s, he decided to lead a group of investors to buy the Yankees from the Columbia Broadcasting System (CBS). He quickly became known for his impatience and then for breaking the law. He fired 20 managers in his first 23 years (he fired one manager, Billy Martin, five times). In 1974, he pleaded guilty to making illegal contributions to President Richard Nixon's re-election campaign (during the Watergate era), and he was suspended from baseball for nine

switch-hitting and fielding skills. His batting average climbed to .289, and his on-base percentage rose from .333 in 1993 to .384 in 1994. Many baseball insiders now think that on-base percentage is a key to winning games, more than pure batting

☆ ☆ ☆ ☆ ☆

months. President Ronald Reagan pardoned Steinbrenner in 1989, in one of the very last acts of his presidency.

In 1990, Steinbrenner was banned from baseball for life for paying a private investigator $40,000 to find harmful secrets about outfielder Dave Winfield. Winfield had sued Steinbrenner about some of the terms in Winfield's Yankee contract. When fans in Yankee Stadium heard of the banishment over their transistor radios, they stood and cheered. They had been starving for a successful team. Steinbrenner was reinstated in 1993, but during his three-year absence, the organization became more patient and minor-league players were able to develop and not be traded for established players. Bernie Williams is often cited as the best example of a Yankee player who was helped by Steinbrenner's absence.

On October 20, 1990, Steinbrenner showed a lighter side of himself on *Saturday Night Live*. In one sketch, he dreamed of a Yankee team on which he manages, coaches, and plays all the positions. Steinbrenner was caricatured in the television comedy *Seinfeld* when the character George Costanza worked with the Yankees. *Seinfeld* co-creator Larry David was the voice of Steinbrenner, who talked nonstop and never listened. His face was never shown.

As of January 2005, Steinbrenner became the most senior of all baseball owners and still the most visible and controversial. He has said, "I will never have a heart attack. I give them."

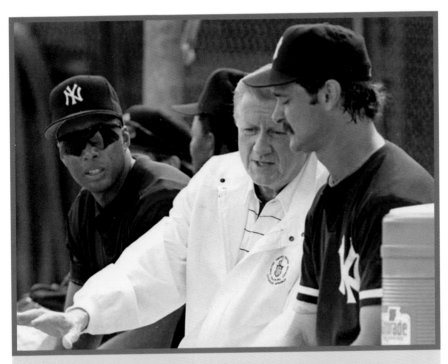

New York Yankees owner George Steinbrenner spoke with Yankee captain Don Mattingly on April 10, 1995, at the team's training facility in Fort Lauderdale, Florida. Next to them was Bernie Williams. Before the 1995 season, Steinbrenner had tried to trade Williams, but manager Buck Showalter persuaded the owner not to do so.

average. Runs win games, and the greater number of times a runner reaches base, the better the chances he will score. Williams scored only 67 runs in 1993 but scored 80 in 1994.

Despite two solid years in 1993 and 1994, reporters in New York wrote that owner George Steinbrenner was not satisfied with Williams. He did not fit a mold. He was fast but did not steal many bases. His long legs were perfect for track, but for the shorter distances in baseball, he was not as effective a runner. He did not hit as many home runs as a Yankee center fielder traditionally has. His throwing was adequate but not exceptional. He was quiet and reserved, and Steinbrenner was not. Steinbrenner reportedly looked to make a trade before the 1995 season. Showalter persuaded him to hold off. Showalter saw some of himself in Williams—he knew that Williams was not a brash and demonstrative player, but he also knew that Williams was more driven to be successful than others thought. He protected the player he had known for so long, and future Yankee fans would be grateful.

STANDING OUT: 1995

When reporter Claire Smith visited Puerto Rico after the 1994 season, she found Williams playing center field for Los Arecibo Lobos el Norte, a local team near San Juan. She filed a report that helps describe Williams during this time:

> To understand Bernie Williams's approach to baseball, one need only understand his approach to life. Both are filled with gentle rhythms and poetic flows, refreshing as the soft breezes that buffet the beaches of Puerto Rico. . . . Williams doesn't just play his position defensively. Instead, he paints it the way an artist lovingly paints a canvas. . . . And he doesn't just run around the bases or merely stalk up to home plate, but seems to glide.

In playing winter-league ball, Williams was still trying to make up for the comparative lack of baseball experience he had as a youngster, and he continued to improve every phase of his game. Most baseball fans in Puerto Rico knew that Williams had made a name for himself with the New York Yankees. Children began to follow him wherever he went before and after games. He was becoming a local hero. Williams used his influence with the children to help them. He said to Smith, "I try to get in their minds that not everybody is going to be a big-league baseball player, but that everybody has something that they're really good at. They have to find what that is and give it their best shot."

Williams went into the 1995 season with more confidence, more experience, more strength (he added 10 more pounds of muscle to his now 190-pound frame), and more dedication than ever. He was at a crucial time in his career: Either he would become a full-fledged star, or he would begin to sink into mediocrity and wait to be replaced. Williams had other reasons for wanting to excel: He wanted to ensure his financial future. Waleska was pregnant with their third child, and even though his salary was more than $200,000, they were not wealthy and not yet financially secure.

The 1995 season was the turning point for Williams and the Yankees. He had a long Opening Day home run on April 26, helping the Yankees to an 8-6 win over the Texas Rangers. The crowd in Yankee Stadium was relatively small, a little more than 50,000 people. Some fans were staying away, angered over the baseball strike that canceled the World Series in 1994 and delayed the start of the 1995 season. Soon, though, more fans would begin to follow this team as the Yankees made a play for the postseason for the first time in years. When the Yankees needed him most, in a September drive for the American League wild-card spot, Williams was extraordinary. He hit near .400 for the month, getting two or more hits in many games. The team needed him so much by then that he could not take time off to be at the birth of his third child, Bianca, on September 14. Despite the concerns he may have had about his new child and his wife, his focus remained on the game: He reached base in 18 of his next 25 at-bats. He had become the iron man of the team, never missing games while other key teammates were injured—Wade Boggs, Paul O'Neill, and team captain Don Mattingly were all unable to play for stretches of the 1995 season.

Williams ended the regular season hitting .307, with 18 home runs and 82 runs batted in. His on-base percentage rose to .392, and his slugging percentage (measuring how many

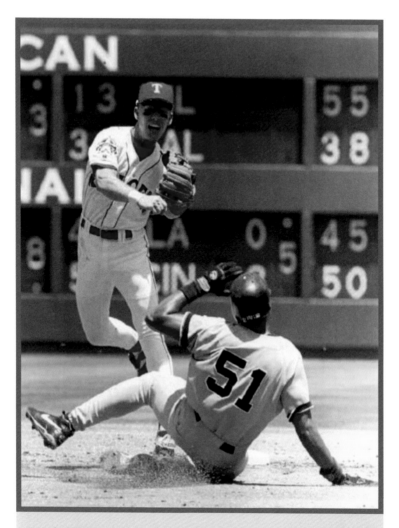

Bernie Williams disrupted the throw of Texas Rangers second baseman Jeff Frye to break up a double play during a game in July 1995 in Arlington, Texas. The 1995 season was Williams's best to date. He hit .307, with 18 home runs and 82 runs batted in.

bases he reached, not just the number of hits) neared .500. He led the team in runs, hits, and total bases. He had arrived as a major leaguer. Over nearly a decade of patient learning,

Williams had developed slowly and surely. He was not an overnight success, but he was now a success by any measure.

The Yankees lost to the Seattle Mariners in the American League Division Series, the first round of the playoffs, but they had come a long way. Reporter Claire Smith had gotten to know Williams more by the end of the season, and she asked him if he had accomplished enough now to feel secure. He answered, as always, with intelligence and insight:

> I don't think I'll ever feel secure; I don't think I can. That's one of the things that keeps me driving, the fact that nothing is for certain. You have to keep improving your game, not only for the team but for yourself. . . . You've got to have a good idea of what you've got to work on and what you want to accomplish, long-term and short-term. Once you have in your mind your goals, you set your work ethic, you go about your job. You play as hard as you can every day, you can't miss with that. You can't be wrong.

UNLIKELY CHAMPIONS OF THE WORLD: 1996

Despite the Yankees' success, manager Buck Showalter was fired at the end of the 1995 season. Many reporters thought that his clashes with Steinbrenner sealed his fate and that, even though he had wisely defended Williams, he had disagreed with the notoriously thin-skinned owner on other issues. He had been proven right often enough to have annoyed his boss. Showalter was replaced by Joe Torre, called "clueless" in some headlines because of his losing record as a manager with other teams. The 1996 Yankees did not have an experienced shortstop, had uneven pitching, and had too many unproven young players to be a preseason favorite. Their best player, team captain Don Mattingly, had retired, and the team had no captain, no leader.

Williams inherited Mattingly's corner locker, which was 50 percent larger than any other locker, but many believed that he was not outgoing enough to assume the leadership role. Torre realized that there are different kinds of leaders. He asked Williams to hit third or fourth in the lineup, meaning he was now the key hitter. Williams responded to these increased expectations with increased performance. He now felt truly important, that he could affect the outcome of each and every game. He realized he liked being relied upon. He was relaxed and confident enough now to help carry a team.

Then the unexpected happened. Not only did a great deal of young talent walk into the Yankee clubhouse all at the same time, but the players also fit well with one another. Rookie Derek Jeter assumed a leadership role even at a very young age, keeping others loose and relaxed with his lively chattering. Paul O'Neill was intensely private, like Williams, but he also liked music, and he and Williams started to perform in the clubhouse together, with O'Neill on drums. Pitcher David Cone liked to talk with Williams about politics and world events, always aware that Williams would know more than most about any issue. Tino Martinez and Williams developed a warm friendship, as did Williams and Jorge Posada.

The Yankees began to win, and win consistently. Each player contributed at just the right time. Williams had five hits in an extra-inning game against the Baltimore Orioles on May 1, a game that lasted almost six hours. The Yankees outlasted the Orioles that day, winning in the fifteenth inning, and set the tone for the rest of the season. On May 27, Williams came back from nagging shoulder injuries and had another five-hit game, leading the Yankees over the Anaheim Angels, 16-5. By the time Williams drove in eight runs against the Detroit Tigers on September 12, he had proven to the team and the fans that he was one of the league's most productive hitters.

The Yankees won the American League East and beat the Texas Rangers in the American League Division Series (ALDS). Williams was a key contributor: He hit .467 with three home runs and five runs batted in, many of them at crucial times.

What happened next will forever be a part of the Williams legend in New York.

When the Yankees faced the Baltimore Orioles for the 1996 American League Championship Series (ALCS), they were not expected to win. In the crucial first game at Yankee Stadium, Derek Jeter hit a famous game-tying home run in the eighth inning. Jeter's long fly ball was deflected by fan Jeffrey Maier, who was leaning over the wall trying to catch the ball, and the hit was incorrectly ruled a home run. Three tense innings later, Williams delivered the most significant home run hit in Yankee Stadium in many years when he led off the eleventh inning with a line drive out of the park off pitcher Randy Myers. As Williams glided around the bases, the Yankee fans cheered louder than they had in many years. The Yankees had won a very big game, 5-4, and the tide turned.

In Game 3, Williams hit a single in the eighth inning that scored Jeter, tying the game, 2-2. Next up was Tino Martinez, who hit a double, and Williams got to third safely. The throw from the outfield came to third baseman Todd Zeile, who spun around to make a throwing motion to second. The ball slipped out of his hand and rolled toward shortstop Cal Ripken. Ripken grabbed the dropped ball and would have thrown Williams out at home plate if Williams had hesitated a split second. Instead, Williams put his speed into some kind of overdrive and would not be denied. He made a perfectly fluid slide into home, popped up, and pumped his fist. He lifted the entire team. They knew they could win the game now. And they did. The news media were in a frenzy after the game, wanting to interview Williams; they looked everywhere for him. Instead of seeking attention, he was quietly lying on the trainer's table after receiving a massage. His eyes closed, he had found a way to detach himself from the swarming reporters. He wanted the team to have the glory, not himself.

Bernie Williams, with his youngest daughter, Bianca, celebrated after the Yankees won the 1996 American League Championship Series over the Baltimore Orioles. The Yankees would go on to win the World Series that year, as well. In the championship series, Williams batted .474 and was named the series' Most Valuable Player.

Williams went on to hit an astounding .474 against the Orioles in the five-game series. When he was not getting a big hit, he was running into walls and jumping above them to take away big hits from the Orioles. One sign in right field at Yankee Stadium read "#51: Superman." Williams was named the Most Valuable Player of the American League Championship Series. When his mother and father saw him hold the trophy above his head, they cried with joy. Orioles manager Davey Johnson told reporters, "We tried everything, but I really don't know how you get him out. He's a special player. He's taken it to another level." Yankees coach Willie Randolph, who went on to become the manager of the New York Mets in 2005, said that the Yankee organization's view of Williams changed after that series. No one wondered any longer if Williams could handle the pressure of a big game. No one would again whisper that he did not seem focused enough or that he was distancing himself from others after a game. When the Yankees went on to win the World Series by beating the Atlanta Braves, Williams became a New York hero. Manager Joe Torre compared him to tennis player Arthur Ashe, another athlete with a quiet composure who made winning a habit.

Williams, Derek Jeter, Mariano Rivera, Tino Martinez, David Cone, Jorge Posada, Andy Pettitte, and other Yankees had all won together—giving the team its first title since 1978. All of them would be remembered forever by Yankee fans as the core of one of the most likable and revered championship dynasties in the history of sports. When they rode through the "Canyon of Heroes" in Lower Manhattan for a ticker-tape parade in their honor on a chilly late-October day, they were thrilled. Williams said he had never seen anything like it, not even in the movies. Millions of Yankees fans showed how much their team meant to them as they pressed forward for a view of their heroes, shouting their approval and praise from office windows and sidewalks. With the World Trade Center towers looming over all of the celebrations that day, none of the players knew that their championship reign was only beginning.

Reigning Champions: 1997–2000

Bernie Williams and several other Yankees became celebrities overnight after the 1996 World Championship. Derek Jeter met up with singer Mariah Carey and began to lead a very high-profile bachelor life in Manhattan. Tino Martinez and Jorge Posada now attracted crowds in airports. Williams went on Conan O'Brien's late-night television show and played his guitar. On November 11, 1996, he made his professional debut as a musician, at the Bottom Line in Greenwich Village in New York City. He said he was more nervous performing before 500 people on center stage than he was in front of 60,000 people at Yankee Stadium. Singer Pete Droge and Williams performed such songs as "The House of the Rising Sun," and Droge said to reporters after the performance that Williams "smoked," which was very high praise. Williams thought that he needed

Bernie Williams posed with an electric guitar before a 1996 game against the Orioles at Camden Yards in Baltimore. He made his professional debut as a musician in 1996 at the Bottom Line in New York City's Greenwich Village neighborhood. "One comparison between playing baseball and playing the guitar is the work ethic," Williams told a reporter.

more work, and he reflected on the similarities between playing guitar and playing baseball when he spoke to sports reporter Ira Berkow:

> One comparison between playing baseball and playing the guitar is the work ethic. To be good, you have to be disciplined in both. In baseball, you practice and practice to get a quality at-bat, hitting the ball level and getting good wood on it. But in baseball, you get more than one chance to hit in a game. The difference in performing in music is that all your mistakes have to be made in practice. You only get one shot when you're on stage.

Williams went on to say that hitting and playing guitar both require a combination of gentleness and aggressiveness. Hitting a Roger Clemens 95-mile-per-hour (153-kilometer-per-hour) fastball is different from hitting a Tim Wakefield 75-mile-per-hour (121-kilometer-per-hour) knuckleball. For one, he has to be aggressive. For the other, he has to wait. Suddenly, everyone seemed interested in what Williams thought. The introvert was becoming just extroverted enough to make reporters in New York want to capture his every word. A champion has many friends.

THE BUMP IN THE CHAMPIONSHIP ROAD: 1997

Ever since he had been with the Yankees, Williams was only able to get a one-year contract for each season. He had never wanted to be a holdout for more money. Even though he was now a star on a championship team, he and his agent, Scott Boras, still accepted a one-year, $5.25 million deal for 1997. Reporter Harvey Araton interviewed Williams on February 20, the first day of spring training that year, at Legends Field in Tampa, Florida. Araton filed this report:

> The star center fielder of the World Series champion New
> York Yankees made his first spring training appearance
> yesterday and what a bore he turned out to be. Didn't
> come swaggering through the clubhouse door with a cigar
> the size of a Louisville slugger between his lips. Didn't get
> involved in friendly but noisy horse play with Tim Raines
> and several others. Didn't require a morning news confer-
> ence to state the nature of his demands for 500 at-bats or
> a contract extension or additional hot dishes for the club-
> house buffet. . . . The man who demands no attention is the
> man who deserves the most.

Williams felt that a long-term contract would not neces-
sarily be best for him at this stage in his career. He was still
getting better, and he did not want to put even more pressure
on himself.

In 1997, Williams had his best year so far in many ways. He
batted .328, hit 21 home runs, and drove in 100 runs. His on-
base percentage improved from .391 in 1996 to .408 in 1997,
and his slugging percentage improved from .535 in 1996 to
.544 in 1997. His fielding percentage (the number of fielding
chances without errors divided by the total number of fielding chances) improved as well, from .986 to .993. Along with
Derek Jeter, he was the hitter whom opposing pitchers feared
the most. He did strike out more in 1997, however, and received
fewer bases on balls. Both are signs of impatience. He needed
to work on that.

The Yankees did not win the American League East. They
won the race for the wild card but faltered in the first round
of the playoffs, losing to the Cleveland Indians. Many fans
complained that the Yankees had fallen far below their 1996
performance, but a closer look reveals that the 1997 Yankees
were just as good in most ways as the 1996 team. The 1997 team
actually won more games, scored 20 more runs, and allowed 99

Throughout his early major-league years, Bernie Williams continued to improve his fielding. Here, he leapt high against the left-center field wall to rob Alex Rodriguez, then with the Seattle Mariners, of a home run during a game in August 1997.

fewer runs. The Baltimore Orioles and Cleveland Indians just improved more than the Yankees did. Still, the Yankees organization became frustrated after the 1997 season, and many reports suggested that they tried to trade Williams to the Detroit Tigers for two pitchers. Someone stopped the deal before it was finalized, and Williams remained a Yankee. Assuming that Williams knew he was the subject of trade talks, the incident must have hurt. The Yankees under George Steinbrenner were known for their insistence on winning championships each and every year, and even players like Williams were not "untouchables." For the Yankees, every play, every inning, every game is magnified by the extraordinary number of media representatives covering each game. There was no place to hide, and New York was a painful place to lose.

Williams, as always, stayed composed in public. He also kept his perspective on what was truly important. He became the Yankees' representative to the Children's Health Fund in 1997. The fund provides health care for impoverished children. Like Derek Jeter with his Turn 2 Foundation, Williams was aware that his new status and visibility made him even more responsible for helping others. Jeter and Williams personified the new Yankees—self-sacrificing, hard-working, and poised in pursuit of perfection.

BACK TO THE TOP: 1998

The 1998 Yankees were a team for the ages. By the end of May, they were 37–13 and 7½ games ahead of the Boston Red Sox. David Wells pitched the thirteenth perfect game (no runs, no hits, and no walks allowed) in major-league history against the Twins on May 17, and Williams won the game with three hits, including a home run. On May 19, the tension between the Yankees and their rivals the Baltimore Orioles boiled over. Williams hit a key eighth-inning home run against Baltimore relief pitcher Armando Benítez, who struck the next batter in the back as a kind of retaliation. Tino Martinez, the player who was hit by the pitch, charged the mound, and a wild brawl that lasted for several minutes broke out. Five players were ejected from the game, and some were suspended, but many fans could feel that the Yankees' intensity of 1996 was back.

Williams injured his knee sliding into second base against the Montreal Expos on June 10, but he was back in the lineup later in the month. On September 4, Williams hit two home runs and drove in four runs as the Yankees beat the Chicago White Sox, 11-6. The win was the Yankees' 100th of the season, the quickest that any American League team had reached that coveted win total. The frustration of the 1997 season seemed to have been transformed into an obsession for winning each and every game.

Williams fielded brilliantly at times and was consistent as the number-four hitter. He provided stability to the lineup. When a team has a great year, it usually means that the lineup has not been juggled every day. Pitching, too, is always a key to such success, and the pitching from David Wells, David Cone, and reliever Mariano Rivera was superb. By the end of the regular season, the team had won 114 games and lost only 48. They had the second-best winning percentage in major-league history. The team hit 207 home runs, the second-most in Yankees history. Eight Yankees hit more than 15 homers, including Williams with 26. They won with both power and controlled hitting. They took a lot of pitches and so made the opposing pitchers work hard. They wore teams down. They won many games even before they came on the field. They were that intimidating.

Williams worked at every aspect of his game and corrected his flaws one by one. His batting average improved in 1998 to .339, his on-base percentage improved to .422, and his slugging percentage rose to .575. His fielding improved as well. Williams had sometimes been criticized for not tracking line drives as well as other center fielders, letting them drop for a hit despite his speed. He made progress in that area, too.

The Yankees faced the Texas Rangers in the first round of the 1998 playoffs, and the pitchers held the Rangers to one run in the three-game sweep of the series. The Yankees then faced the very tough Cleveland Indians, who had been to the World Series the year before. The Yankees won in a close and tough six-game series, with Williams getting some key hits and making some important plays in center field.

Yankee Stadium on a late October evening for a World Series game is a very special place. Some of the richest and most famous people in the world gather to see and be seen. In 1998, Jack Nicholson, Bruce Willis, Barbara Walters, and Sarah Michelle Gellar were just a few of the more visible fans at the opening game. It was the thirty-fifth World Series for

☆ ☆ ☆ ☆ ☆ ☆

THE WORLD SERIES RING

Championship rings have become serious pieces of "bling," more portable trophies than simply pieces of jewelry. It was not always so. The New York Giants celebrated their 1922 World Series victory by giving each player a small ring. They were the first team to offer a ring as a reward. Before that, teams had usually given pocket watches to their champions. Rings remained relatively small until football's Super Bowl was inaugurated in 1967, and then ring sizes and values exploded. A competition to have the biggest and best ring was off and running.

The Balfour Company has made most of the New York Yankees' championship rings. One of its rivals is Jostens, which was chosen to make the 2004 championship ring for the Boston Red Sox. Balfour has made 25 rings for the Yankees. Jostens has made one for the Red Sox. Both companies have to create several sample rings before a final design is accepted. Before 1968, each baseball team owned the rights to the design of its ring. After 1968, Major League Baseball tried to take more control of the ring-design process.

Some sports-collectibles experts think that the 1998 Yankees' World Series Championship ring set a new standard for baseball rings. The ring is made of gold and has 48 high-quality diamonds set in a blue stone. The famous interlocking "N" and

the Yankees, and only the second for their opponents, the San Diego Padres. A grand slam by Tino Martinez beat the Padres in Game 1, Scott Brosius was the Yankees' hitting hero in Game 3, and Williams and pitcher Andy Pettitte led the way in Game 4. The Yankees swept the Padres, and were once again world champions. In the visitors' clubhouse in Qualcomm

"Y" logo of the Yankees is in the middle, and the sides of the ring read "125–50" and "Best Ever" and "Tradition." The ring is valued near $30,000. Others say that the 2004 Red Sox ring sets the standard for collectible value. It has 1.89 carats of small diamonds, and two carats of rubies that make up the "B." The ring says, "Greatest Comeback in History" and "8 Straight Wins."

Teams now tend to make two classes of rings for a championship, an "on-field" ring and an "executive/administrative" ring. The first is for the players, coaches, and managers. The second, somewhat smaller, is for the other members of the organization. Sometimes it gets confusing when a ring goes up for sale—which "class" of ring is it, or is it a replica or sample?

Jose Canseco asked $40,000 when he put his 2000 Yankees championship ring (he was with the team for 37 games in 2000 and struck out in his one World Series at-bat) up for sale on his Web site. The ring was advertised as having 22 diamonds and weighing 34.5 grams. The ring was soon taken off the Web site, and some say a California collector bought the ring. In July 2006, a Red Sox championship ring was placed on eBay by a former Red Sox employee who had student loans to pay off. He is asking $100,000, and reportedly diehard Sox fan Stephen King has been interested.

Stadium in San Diego, the 1989 Perrier-Jouet Brut champagne flowed for hours, with even Steinbrenner getting doused.

Counting the postseason, the 1998 Yankees won 125 games while only losing 50, a major-league record for most wins in a season. They hit home runs, but they ran out slow ground balls for hits as well. They respected other teams and refused to be loud and boastful. They took on the characteristics of their best players—Derek Jeter, Bernie Williams, Tino Martinez, and Paul O'Neill. They joined the other legendary teams of baseball: the 1927 Yankees with Babe Ruth and Lou Gehrig; the 1961 Yankees with Mickey Mantle, Roger Maris, Whitey Ford, and Yogi Berra; the 1976 Cincinnati Reds with Joe Morgan, Pete Rose, Johnny Bench, and Tony Pérez. The 1998 Yankees were as good as any of those teams, especially when Bernie Williams was more Bronx Bomber than Bronx Bambi.

With his .339 average, Williams won the American League batting title in 1998. He also won a Gold Glove award, given to the best fielder at each position as voted on by other players, managers, and sportswriters. With his 1998 World Series Championship ring, Williams became the first player in major-league history to win a Gold Glove, a batting title, and the World Series in the same year. He was seventh in the balloting for the American League Most Valuable Player award. He was now recognized as one of the best all-around players in baseball history, and he was about to become one of the richest.

SIGNING FOR THE LONG TERM

The long series of one-year contracts was going to end. Williams and his agent, Scott Boras, felt that the Yankees had to open their checkbook after his 1998 performance with a championship team. They were right. The Yankees, though, did not make it easy, and other teams wanted to steal Williams away.

On November 23, 1998, the Boston Red Sox offered Williams a seven-year, $91.5 million contract. He met and liked the Red

Sox manager, Jimy Williams. Signing with the archrival Red Sox would be odd, though, and Bernie Williams thought he might have to become more of a vocal leader. The Arizona Diamondbacks also made him an offer, and Williams sensed that they were a rising team that would win the World Series within a few years (he was right). His heart, however, was still with the Yankees, and he hoped that they could match or at least come close to the Red Sox's or Diamondbacks' offers. Williams believed that he deserved a contract that would once and for all make his family financially secure. It had been more than 13 years since he first signed for $16,000 in 1985, and he had proven over and over his worth to the team. He was a loyal Yankee and always had been.

On November 24, Williams and Boras met with Steinbrenner and Yankees general manager Brian Cashman. They met in a conference room at the Yankees complex in Tampa; the room had blue walls with framed pictures of Yankees players and two overhead fans that never stopped whirring. Steinbrenner had always been distant to Williams, never quite believing that Williams was the Yankee center fielder who would help the team win many World Championships. As Williams calmly described the other two offers, he said he wanted to remain a Yankee but he also wanted to be treated fairly. He was rational and persuasive, but he also opened up about how much the Yankees meant to him. He did something he rarely does—he showed all of the emotions that drive him.

Steinbrenner responded to Williams positively and said he needed to think. What happened after that meeting is unknown to all but a few. The speculation later was that Steinbrenner and the Yankees wanted options and tried to offer a contract to Cleveland Indians slugger Albert Belle. Others think Steinbrenner realized that he had been wrong about Williams and that he had to pay more than he was planning for the center fielder. He had underestimated Williams from the start, as overbearing and aggressive people often do when dealing with gentler and quieter people.

When Williams boarded a flight to Puerto Rico the next morning, he had heard nothing from Steinbrenner and Cashman. He had poured his heart out, and he had not slept that night. He thought his days with the Yankees were over. Waleska Williams told a reporter later, "I saw the pain in his eyes when he came back. That's the saddest I've seen this man in eight years." Just after 2 P.M. on November 25, the Williamses' phone rang. Scott Boras told Williams that he was now the highest-paid player in Yankee history— $87.5 million over seven years. Williams was ecstatic and shouted, "Yeah, yeah, yeah." When Boras called later that day, Waleska told him that Williams was in another room, alone, playing his guitar. She said he had a contented look on his face. He was playing the blues, lost in a world far away from baseball and money.

NUMBER THREE: 1999

After signing his new contract, the Williamses bought a house in Armonk, New York, so their three children could be close to their father during the season. For years, Waleska and the children would visit New York but return to Puerto Rico, and long separations made life difficult for the whole family. Some friends sensed that being apart so often had taken its toll on Williams and his wife, and that would now change. The family could feel closer to each other in many ways. Waleska was concerned about taking her children away from their relatives and grandparents in Puerto Rico, but when they became involved in dance, gymnastics, and chess clubs in their new hometown, she thought they had made the right decision. Bernie Alexander, Beatriz Noemi, and Bianca all seemed happier, as did their father.

Reporters often asked Williams questions about how being rich had changed him. Williams replied to writer Buster Olney that he had not changed much, even though he now drove a Mercedes:

> The game is no different, playing and preparing for it. I've been doing it so long, it doesn't change because of the contract. The joy and sorrow of playing through the year is a whole world within itself. What's going to happen in a year is going to happen no matter what, no matter how much money you're making. I think it really helps to keep myself in check, making sure I'm the same player and the same person, because it doesn't really have to change.

Williams's statistics demonstrated that his play improved after signing the contract that made him rich. Incredibly, he seemed to get better every single year and in almost every category used to measure performance. His 1999 batting average was .342, even higher than his best-in-league in 1998. His all-important on-base percentage continued to rise, to .435. He continued to hit home runs, and his 115 RBIs was his personal best. On October 2, he received his 100th walk. He became the first Yankee since Lou Gehrig to get at least 200 hits and 100 walks in a season, and the first major leaguer since Stan Musial in 1953. Such a feat is incredible because players with many hits tend not to have that many walks, and players who walk a lot tend not to have that many hits. Williams was now in rare company, and was being compared to the players who had monuments in center field at Yankee Stadium.

The 1999 Yankees had to endure as much personal loss as any team in recent memory. Manager Joe Torre was diagnosed with prostate cancer, Darryl Strawberry battled colon cancer and drug addiction, Scott Brosius's father died suddenly during the season, as did Luis Sojo's. When Paul O'Neill was told that his father had died of a heart attack, he was so weakened by grief that his teammates had to keep him from falling. The personal tragedies made the team even closer.

Bernie Williams is not always shy and reserved. During Game 1 of the American League Championship Series in 1999, he jumped into the air as he got to home plate after hitting a tenth-inning home run. His homer gave the Yankees a 4-3 victory over the Boston Red Sox.

The team won all of its postseason games except one. In the very first game of the playoffs on October 5, Williams single-handedly demolished the Texas Rangers with a single, a double, and a home run, driving in six runs. Perhaps the most pivotal game came against archrival Boston. In Game 1 of the American

League Championship Series, on October 13, Williams led off the bottom of the tenth inning with the score tied, 3-3. He was facing Rod Beck, one of the most feared closing pitchers in baseball. During the season, Beck had thrown an inside fastball on Williams that broke his bat in half. Williams, like Tiger Woods, has an incredible memory, and he uses his memory to sort through what may occur in a game. Williams expected another inside fastball from Beck since the pitch had worked so well before. It came, and Williams hit it over the center-field wall of Yankee Stadium. When he saw the ball clear the wall, he pumped his fist twice and then jumped into a crowd of delirious teammates. The 57,181 witnesses were out of their seats, and many were out of their minds with joy. Joe Torre later said, "Bernie does big things." The Yankees went on to beat Boston, four games to one, for the American League pennant, and they swept the Atlanta Braves in the World Series. The Yankees were world champions again, for the second year in a row and the third time in four years. They were making it look easy.

A DYNASTY CROWNED: 2000

Williams had been playing in more pain than most of his teammates and even his family knew. His shoulders and his knees had been a constant source of discomfort, and Williams met with team doctors after the 1999 season to discuss the possibility of an operation on his shoulder. They decided that the risk of a long recovery was too great and that, if Williams could bear the pain, he should. He did, however, have laser surgery on his eyes, to improve his vision so he could get rid of the glasses and contact lenses he had worn since he was young. The Yankees had concerns about the eye surgery, but Williams went ahead. The surgery went well, and Williams reported that he could see better than ever. That was not good news for American League pitchers.

On April 23 in a game against the Toronto Blue Jays, Williams hit two home runs, one from each side of the plate.

Jorge Posada, the switch-hitting Yankee catcher, did the same, the first time in major-league history that teammates accomplished that in the same game. On June 17 against the White Sox, Williams drove in seven runs with a single, two doubles, and a home run. By the 2000 All-Star Game, Williams was hitting .329 and had driven in 80 runs, putting him on pace to rival Yankee great Joe DiMaggio's 1937 season total of 167 RBIs. His batting average was the highest on the team when runners were in scoring position with two outs: .381. During one stretch just before the All-Star break, he scored at least one run in 13 straight games. He was carrying the team. Williams had made yet another important adjustment. Teams had noticed that, when he was batting left-handed, he could be gotten out with high fastballs. He worked on this weakness and overcame it. High fastballs were now flying out of the park when he batted left-handed. Williams was more consistent than ever as a switch-hitter. Often, he had started the season slowly when batting left-handed, since it was not his natural side, and he needed time to build his proficiency. By 2000, he had corrected his slow starts.

The team itself started slowly in 2000, and by the All-Star break, it had lost almost as many games as it had won. Then, in early August, the team seemed to throw a switch and turn on a winning streak, capturing 22 of 31 games at one point. The Yankees ended up finishing first in the American League East with a record of 87–74. They beat the Oakland Athletics in the American League Division Series and the Seattle Mariners in the American League Championship Series. In the crucial third game of the championship series, Williams and Tino Martinez hit back-to-back home runs to give the Yankees the lead. They then faced the New York Mets in the 2000 World Series, a "Subway Series." Williams hit a crucial home run in the final game, on October 26, and the Yankees won the game, 4-2, and the World Series, four games to one. The last out of the game, and the World Series, was a long fly ball from Mets catcher Mike Piazza that Williams caught. Williams dropped

Bernie Williams held up the 2000 World Series trophy after the Yankees defeated their crosstown rivals, the New York Mets, in five games. The series ended when Mike Piazza hit a fly ball to Williams for an out. The Yankees had now won three World Series in a row and four of the last five.

to one knee in prayer and thanks. Williams still has the ball at home, signed by most of his teammates. It is one of his more cherished possessions.

With the World Series victory, the Yankees were the first team to win three World Series in a row since the Oakland A's, who won the title from 1972 to 1974. The Yankees had won four out of the last five World Championships, a string only rivaled by the greatest teams in sports, such as the Pittsburgh Steelers of football in the mid-to-late 1970s and the Boston Celtics of basketball in the late 1950s and the 1960s. Many Yankee fans saw no reason that the championship streak could not continue for many more years. They had become addicted to winning.

Only Near Greatness: 2001–2006

When Bernie Williams signs autographs, he signs them with the letters "SDG" below his name. The letters stand for "Solo Dios Gloria," a Spanish phrase praising God. Faith is a constant in Williams's life, and he and Waleska have joined Catholic churches wherever they have lived. Waleska was even in the church choir during their years in Albany. Williams's faith is intensely personal to him. Like many professional athletes who have been blessed with such extraordinary physical gifts, he has been grateful and cannot simply believe it was DNA roulette that made him so fortunate.

On April 9, 2001, Williams received a phone call from his brother, Hiram, that their 73-year-old father was being taken to a hospital in Bayamón, Puerto Rico. Mr. Williams had pulmonary fibrosis, a horrible disease that slowly breaks down the lungs and scars them. Speaking and breathing become hard work. Williams left the Yankees immediately, and when he arrived to see his father, he broke down and cried. His father was fighting for every breath. Williams told a reporter, "What this has taught me is that there are a lot of things I cannot control. I can have all the money in the world, and I cannot get my dad better. Sometimes you have to let go and pray."

Williams said that he could not stop thinking about all the times he had spent with his father, who had been strong and fearless and the one person in whom Williams could confide. A few weeks later, Mr. Williams died. Williams and his family were devastated. Their grief took them far away from thoughts of baseball, but Williams soon had to return to the Yankees.

WORLD TRAGEDY AND NEAR TRIUMPH: 2001

The loss of his father took its toll on Williams, and his hitting was well below average during the first half of the season. In early May, he was hitting .215; by mid-June, his average was back up to .300. The Yankees had won three straight World Championships, but time was starting to affect the team's veterans.

Then, on September 11, 2001, two hijacked commercial airliners were flown into the World Trade Center, killing almost 3,000 people. Almost 200 more people were killed when another hijacked airliner struck the Pentagon in Virginia, and more died when a fourth hijacked plane crashed in a field in Pennsylvania. New York and the country were in shock. At first, the baseball season seemed insignificant. Then, resuming a new kind of "normal" life seemed very significant for the residents of New York City. The city, led by its mayor, Rudolph Giuliani, threw its heart into the Yankees' postseason. Everyone wanted to divert themselves, however temporarily, from the deadening grief and rumble of terror that surrounded the city and the country.

The young Oakland Athletics beat the Yankees in Yankee Stadium in the first two games of the American League Division

Bernie Williams and Seattle pitcher Jamie Moyer watched as Williams's hit left the ballpark in the first inning of Game 3 of the 2001 American League Championship Series. Williams also had a key home run in Game 5 of the series, helping the Yankees win the American League pennant.

Series, a best-of-five series. No team had ever come back from losing its first two games at home. The Yankees clawed back to win a pitcher's duel in Game 3 in Oakland, highlighted by a spectacular Derek Jeter defensive play. In Game 4 on October 14, Williams took over. He drove in five runs and almost singlehandedly tied the series at two games apiece. The Yankees won the fifth game and advanced to play the Seattle Mariners in the American League Championship Series. Williams's home run fueled a rally in the fifth and final game of the championship series, and the Yankees advanced to the 2001 World Series.

Going into the 2001 World Series, the Yankees had a record of 16 wins and 3 losses in the last four World Series they had played. Even though Williams had been an outstanding player in each of the four American League Championship Series before those World Series, batting .360, he had been less successful in the World Series games, hitting only three home runs, driving in eight runs, and batting .141. But, he now had 16 postseason home runs, passing Babe Ruth in that category among all players. Again, Williams had his troubles in this World Series, batting .208 with only one RBI. The Arizona Diamondbacks won the first two games of the 2001 World Series behind their ace pitchers, Curt Schilling and Randy Johnson. The Yankees came back and won the next three games, all at Yankee Stadium. All were thrilling games won in the late innings on dramatic hits from Derek Jeter, Tino Martinez, and Scott Brosius. Game 4 and Game 5 were both won after two-out two-run home runs tied the games in the ninth inning. The Diamondbacks won the final two games and the World Series, coming from behind in the ninth inning of the seventh game, the first team ever to win a World Series after being behind in the ninth inning of the final game. The home team won every game. The 2001 World Series has been called the most exciting Series in modern times, and even though the Yankees lost, the team returned home as heroes. They had given New York a welcome relief from fear and loss.

Williams had the identical batting average in 2001 as he had in 2000—.307. His on-base percentage improved in 2001 to .395, but his slugging percentage dropped to .522 from .566 in 2000. His fielding had been superb both years; in 2000, he had a perfect fielding percentage of 1.000. In 2001, the percentage dropped, but only slightly, to .994. Many consider these two years to have been his best in the field. Overall, most experts consider his best hitting years to have been from 1997 to 1999, when his three-year average was an astounding .336. He now had four World Series rings, a batting title, four Gold Glove awards, and five All-Star Game appearances. Williams had had more obvious success than most players in major-league history. Even though his peak years appeared to be behind him as he headed into the 2002 season, he was still better than most center fielders in the majors.

Younger players had grown up admiring Williams, especially his approach to hitting. Reporter Buster Olney wrote in 2001 about Williams's thoughts on the art of hitting a baseball:

> A hitter's head is littered with thought, drawn from dog-eared pages of mental notes. He knows from scouting reports what the pitcher likes to throw. . . . He remembers: don't chase that high fastball, don't get behind in the count, don't let your front shoulder fly open, don't be too aggressive, don't be too passive. . . . When Williams comes to bat . . . [he] steps away from home plate and clears his mind. Relax. See the ball coming out of the pitcher's hand. Relax. Hit the ball up the middle. . . . He will not be rushed at the plate. . . . Williams sees the pitch leaving the pitcher's hand. His mind is uncluttered. His front foot taps back and punches forward, and his hands and the bat are moving, in rhythm.

That method of hitting has served Williams well, and it is what he tries to teach at baseball clinics. He tries to prepare, but not to overthink. Concentration and relaxation are the alternating currents in his performance. They ebb and flow through him. He has learned well, and can now teach others.

LESS SUCCESS: 2002

On March 6, 2002, Williams sat in the dugout at Legends Field in Tampa during spring training and watched Derek Jeter sign some autographs for minor leaguers. He then patted Jeter on the stomach and asked if he was 25 yet. Jeter (almost 28 years old) asked if Williams was going to shine his shaved head. The clubhouse teasing was normal, but the mood in the clubhouse was not. The Yankees were changing. They had to start the season without proven veterans like Scott Brosius, Paul O'Neill, and Tino Martinez, who had all left or retired. Jeter and Williams were now the two most visible team leaders, but Williams was not about to change his quiet style and start organizing team meetings. He was not going to change his habit of avoiding postgame news conferences; he thought they provided too many chances for making excuses or grabbing attention. Yankees manager Joe Torre may have wanted Williams to become more publicly vocal with a new set of players, but Williams was going to stay the same: "Once I stepped between those lines, I gave it my best shot. That's one of the things a leader is about. No matter the circumstances or adversities, you're going to give it your best shot. And don't give any excuses." But with the absence of the influential and experienced Brosius, O'Neill, and Martinez, the rare set of conditions that led to four World Championships was breaking up.

Williams started the 2002 season slowly, and he had to get cortisone shots in each of his shoulders to help control arthritis. As of May 4, he was batting .243, with two home runs and only eight RBIs over the first 31 games. Then he did something unexpected. He asked the Yankees' scoreboard operators to stop

Yankee third-base coach Willie Randolph congratulated Bernie Williams after his three-run homer in the first game of the 2002 American League Division Series against the Anaheim Angels. Although the Yankees won that game, they lost the series to the Angels. It was the first time since 1997 that the Yankees would not be appearing in the World Series.

playing music when he came to the plate. Each Yankee had a favorite recording artist and song that the scoreboard operators played as the player was coming to bat and digging his spikes into the dirt of the batter's box. Derek Jeter had Jay-Z. Robin Ventura had the Red Hot Chili Peppers. Rondell White had Nelly. Williams had Prince. Beginning on May 5, Williams became the only Yankee to be greeted with silence when he came to bat. Although he had always blocked out the world when he batted, some part of him had also always heard the music. Stopping the music worked wonders. Williams batted .352 with 17 home runs and 94 RBIs in the 122 games after the music died.

The Yankees won the American League East, as they had done every year since 1998, and they faced the Anaheim Angels in the American League Division Series. In the first game at Yankee Stadium, on October 1, Williams came to bat in the eighth inning with two men on and the score tied, 5-5. The scoreboard operators played no music, but the stands were rocking with the chants of "Ber-nie! Ber-nie!" Angels pitcher Brendan Donnelly, a 31-year-old rookie, was ready to throw a fastball by Williams and get out of the two-out jam. Instead, Williams crushed a three-run home run over the right-field fence, and the Angels were beaten, 8-5. After the game, Derek Jeter said, "You can't explain Bernie." He meant it as a high compliment.

The Yankees, however, fell short of their last few postseason performances. They eventually lost to the Angels. Anaheim was a good and balanced team, and the Angels went on to win the 2002 World Series. The Yankees were disappointed, but most fans felt that Williams had a very good year. He ended up hitting .333, with 19 home runs and 102 RBIs. His on-base percentage of .415 was better than in 2001, and he came in tenth in the balloting for the American League Most Valuable Player award. His slugging percentage, however, fell for the second straight year, to .493. He was losing his strength ever so slowly, just as he had improved it slowly years before.

BACK TO THE WORLD SERIES: 2003

Time was catching up to Williams physically. He underwent knee surgery in 2003 and missed more than 40 games. Williams has estimated that major-league players are 100 percent healthy about 25 percent of the time. The other days are exercises in pain management. Players play hurt, and most of the time fans and reporters never hear about what the trainer knows. Veterans always have to remind younger players that, even if they are not physically pain-free, they must be mentally ready to play every game.

Williams's batting average dropped to .263 in 2003, his lowest since 1991, and his on-base percentage and slugging percentage continued to fall. Williams seemed sluggish at the plate in the first game of the 2003 American League Division Series against the Minnesota Twins. When he made an error in center field that let in two runs, Yankees owner George Steinbrenner could be seen prowling around his seat. In Game 3, Williams let Doug Mientkiewicz's bouncing single skip off his glove for another error, and Steinbrenner was seen slamming his fist on a table.

Williams did make up for his mistakes, however, and had two hits in the crucial Game 3. He hit .400 and had three important runs batted in during the series. All of his hits were important, as were his patient at-bats when he received walks. He did not let his lapses in the field carry over to his hitting. The Yankees beat the Twins, three games to one, and went on to play the Boston Red Sox in one of the most memorable American League Championship Series ever played.

The Yankees and Red Sox played seven intense games in the 2003 championship series. One of the most unforgettable was Game 3, featuring a pitching matchup between Roger Clemens (who had been with the Red Sox most of his career but had signed with the Yankees in the hopes of getting his first World Series ring) and Red Sox ace Pedro Martínez. After Yankee Karim García was hit in the back with a pitch, Clemens retaliated and threw close to Manny Ramírez's head the next inning. Ramírez charged the mound, and the brawl that followed became legendary. Seventy-two-year-old Yankees coach Don

Bernie Williams bobbled a hit during Game 3 of the 2003 American League Division Series against the Minnesota Twins. He made up for his error with his bat, getting two hits in the game. Williams batted .400 during the division series.

Zimmer charged Martínez at one point, and Martínez forced him to the ground. The brawl even spread to the bullpens, where a Red Sox groundskeeper fought with Yankee pitcher Jeff Nelson. For months, the police in Boston investigated who did what to whom and when.

The Yankees won the seventh game when Red Sox manager Grady Little left a tiring Martínez on the mound too long in the eighth inning with the Red Sox ahead, 5-2. Four hits later, the Yankees had tied the game, 5-5. In the bottom of the eleventh inning, Aaron Boone launched a home run into the left-field seats, and the Yankees celebrated as if they had won the World Series. Williams was invisible throughout much of the championship series, hitting .192, but he saved his only good game for last. He collected two hits and a run batted in during the decisive Game 7. He had come through again when his team needed him most.

The Yankees went on to play the Florida Marlins in the 2003 World Series, and they were heavily favored to win their fifth championship in the last eight seasons. The Marlins were a young team and seemingly no match for the Yankee veterans. Williams was no longer invisible and had the best World Series of his career. He hit a home run in Game 1, and in Game 3, he hit a three-run home run to center field in the ninth inning to ensure a Yankee victory. That home run was his nineteenth in postseason play, a new major-league record. Williams also had 65 postseason RBIs, another major-league record. Unfortunately for the Yankees, Marlin pitchers Brad Penny, Dontrelle Willis, and Josh Beckett pitched brilliantly, and the Marlins got just enough hitting to win the World Series in six games. Some thought that the American League Championship Series had taken so much out of the Yankees that they tired against the young Marlins. Game 6 was the 100th World Series game played at Yankee Stadium, and the Marlins became the first opposing team to win a World Series championship at the Stadium since 1981. The loss was a bitter disappointment for Yankee fans. The 2004 season was even worse.

HELPING TO REVERSE THE CURSE: 2004

The Yankees had gone three years without a championship ring, and George Steinbrenner felt it was time to make a bold move. He signed star Alex Rodriguez from the Texas Rangers to play third base. In doing so, he added the most expensive player in team-sports history to play next to Derek Jeter, the second-highest-paid player. The left side of the Yankees infield cost more than five Boeing 737 airplanes. Many fans worried that the new combination would upset the team's balance and chemistry. They may have had good reason to worry.

Williams had a highlight in June, when he recorded his 2,000th career hit, a milestone few major leaguers reach. He went on to hit .262 for the year, with a .360 on-base percentage and a .435 slugging percentage. The on-base percentage was his lowest since 1993, and his slugging percentage showed that he was still losing power, especially when compared with his peak years of 1996 to 2000. It is perhaps no accident that the Yankees' championships coincided perfectly with Williams's best slugging years, and the championship drought afterward mirrored Williams's decline in power.

The Yankees won the American League East Division in 2004 and breezed through the American League Division Series, beating the Minnesota Twins three games to one. Williams collected his twentieth postseason home run in Game 3. When the Yankees took a three-game-to-none lead over the Red Sox in the 2004 American League Championship Series, no one expected what was to happen next. In the ninth inning of Game 4, with the Yankees leading, 4-3, and Mariano Rivera on the mound for the Yankees, one of the most remarkable comebacks in sports history began. Bill Mueller singled in Dave Roberts to tie the game, and David Ortiz hit a walk-off home run in the eleventh inning. The Red Sox went on to win the next three games as well and then swept the St. Louis Cardinals in the 2004 World Series. The Sox became the subject of movies and books celebrating their first World Championship since 1918—ending the so-called Curse of the Bambino (a superstition cited as the reason why the Sox had not won a World Series after selling Babe Ruth to the Yankees). Yankees fans went into mourning.

NEARING THE END OF A BRILLIANT CAREER

At the beginning of the 2005 season, manager Joe Torre made it official: Williams, now 36, was to be a part-time player. He had slowed down enough in the field that he could no longer reach the gaps between center field and left and right fields.

He was now a liability, and his declining power did not make him an ideal number-four hitter any longer. Williams adjusted to his new role with dignity and without any outward signs of bitterness. Still, he did end up playing in 141 games during the season. On August 2, 2005, the Yankees announced that they would not be extending Williams's contract; they could still sign him later for another year, but he was now not a part of their longer-range plans. The 2005 Yankee season ended in a first-round playoff loss to the Los Angeles Angels of Anaheim, and the Yankees' championship drought continued. Williams had his least-productive year, batting .249 and dropping dramatically in on-base percentage (.321) and slugging percentage (.367). His career was nearing its end. Like so many of the best players, he had become a star in his mid-20s and was among the league's best until his mid-30s. As of December 7, 2005, Williams had the longest stay with one team of any player in the American League. He had become the senior member of the American League just when Steinbrenner became the senior owner in baseball.

Williams was thrilled to get the chance to play for Puerto Rico in the first World Baseball Classic (WBC). The WBC was a new international tournament for the best 16 baseball programs in the world, and it was first held in March 2006. Teammates Carlos Delgado, Mike Lowell, Javier Vázquez, and Carlos Beltrán rounded out the stars from Puerto Rico. When Williams came to bat during the first game for Puerto Rico, against Panama, the chants of "Ber-nie, Ber-nie" echoed throughout Hiram Bithorn Stadium in San Juan. When he knocked in the eventual game-winning run, the chants turned to wild cheering. Williams later told reporter Jack Curry, "I feel like I was playing the World Series in March. It was a great feeling. There's something very special about playing for my country, my hometown, people chanting my name." Puerto Rico did well, making it to the second round, but the World Baseball Classic was won by Japan, with Cuba the runner-up.

The Yankees signed Williams to play in 2006, paying him just over $1 million. They had signed former Red Sox outfielder Johnny Damon to play center field. They must have felt that Williams would still be a good insurance policy in case several outfielders were injured in 2006. As it turned out, that is exactly what happened, as Hideki Matsui and Gary Sheffield both had wrist injuries. By playing right field, center field, and designated hitter, Williams helped keep the 2006 Yankees in or near

★ ★ ★ ★ ☆

THE WORLD BASEBALL CLASSIC

Major League Baseball (MLB) envied the Olympics and soccer's World Cup. Baseball had truly become international, and MLB wanted to reflect that in an international tournament. Professional baseball teams could not send their best players to the Olympics because the baseball season was under way whenever the Olympics were held. After years of planning and negotiating with the players' union and owners, MLB announced in May 2005 that the World Baseball Classic (WBC) would be played in March 2006 and again in 2009. After that, the WBC would be held every four years. Major leaguers would play during their spring training and play for their home country.

The 2006 tournament had 16 teams, divided into four pools. Each team played one game against the other three teams in the pool, and the top two in each pool advanced. New pools were formed for Round 2. Again, each team played the other three teams, with the top two moving on to the single-elimination semifinals. The winners of the semifinals played one game for the championship. The tournament structure was borrowed from the World Cup and worked well. Some controversy did arise, however.

first place for most of the season. On June 16, Williams had four hits in five at-bats and crushed a ninth-inning home run to beat the Washington Nationals, 7-5. On June 20, he collected five hits against the Philadelphia Phillies, leading the Yankees to a 9-7 win.

His frustration, however, at not having all the skills he had before began to show. In May, he was thrown out of a major-league game for the first time when he tossed his bat and helmet

☆ ☆ ☆ ☆ ☆

Yankees owner George Steinbrenner publicly worried that his players might get injured. The players' union did not want the drug tests to be the same ones used for the Olympics, which were notoriously thorough and rigorous. MLB found a compromise set of tests that were more comprehensive than MLB's, but less thorough than the Olympics. Cuban players were not allowed to talk to the international media, and they practiced in an area set off from fans by orange rubber cones. Fidel Castro's son was their doctor, and he kept a close eye on what was going on, not wanting any of the players to defect.

Nippon Professional Baseball, the Japanese equivalent of MLB, worried about the timing of the tournament since the season in Japan begins earlier than the MLB season. The league eventually accepted a bid to take part in the WBC, and Japan ended up winning the championship game in San Diego over Cuba, 10-6. Players worldwide reported a particular thrill in playing for their country as opposed to playing for a professional team. Fans in such baseball-crazy countries as South Korea, the Dominican Republic, and Japan all got to see their teams make it to the final four. And, unlike soccer, no game was decided by penalty kicks or head butts.

Bernie Williams talked with a couple of spectators before a game on March 11, 2006, in the World Baseball Classic at Hiram Bithorn Stadium in San Juan, Puerto Rico. Williams had a great time representing his homeland in the tournament. "There's something very special about playing for my country, my hometown, people chanting my name," he said.

after he was called out on strikes. As usual, he made no excuses. He told a reporter afterward, "As much as I think the umpire had a bad day, it doesn't justify my actions."

In June 2006, Williams played in his 2,000th game. He joined 203 other players in baseball history to reach that milestone of endurance. In February 2007, Williams did not accept the Yankees' offer to come to spring training on a minor-league contract and play himself onto the roster if another player got hurt. Instead, he was willing to stay in shape and wait for the Yankees to change their minds and offer him a guaranteed spot on the roster. "As it is right now, it doesn't seem like I am going to be playing with that team this year," he told a reporter.

When Williams made an error or struck out, the Yankee fans did not boo him the way they do many other players. They respect Williams and all he has meant to the team. Williams called this period near the end of his career "a great time in my life," and putting on the Yankee pinstripes still means a great deal to him. He is a beloved player who should find himself in the Baseball Hall of Fame some day. He has earned his reputation for graceful greatness. He has given credit to others, and he has made no excuses. He is the newest Yankee legend.

The
Music Man

Music has been such a part of Bernie Williams's life that he once told a reporter, "Baseball is a good escape from music." His biography on his official Web site is devoted much more to music than to baseball. He has always let music express the feelings he found difficult to convey with words. Williams has always seen similarities between music and baseball, and on his Web site he elaborates on that connection. He also notes how he uses his life as an inspiration for his music:

> Music gives you rhythm, makes things flow; a lot of things you can utilize in baseball having a musical mind. You have coordination, the rhythm, timing. There's nothing better than having everything flowing in the game, and musically speaking, you can compare it to being in the zone, everything

flowing like it's effortless. And it happens in both fields. . . . Every major event that would happen in my life I would try to create a melody, a song that would make me think about that moment.

AN ARTISTIC DEVELOPMENT

Williams's development as a musician has taken a distinct path. His interest started with hearing his father play the Spanish guitar when he was a child, but his academic training at the Free School of Music in San Juan included listening to classical artists like Bach, Mozart, Haydn, and Vivaldi. He was trained on the classical acoustic (that is, non-electric) guitar.

Soon after graduating from high school, Williams picked up an electric guitar in New York and was astounded at the new range of sounds he could produce. He was hooked on experimenting. He worked with a Fender Stratocaster, which gave him more versatility in producing sounds than he could achieve with acoustic guitars. Eventually, Williams also picked up the steel-string guitar, an acoustic guitar with steel strings that create a brighter and louder sound than nylon. It also has more control than an electric guitar.

He began to listen to blues artists, especially Muddy Waters, B.B. King, and Robben Ford. The blues led him to jazz, to Miles Davis, John Coltrane, and Charlie Parker. The newer jazz sounds then took hold of him, and he became influenced by Pat Metheny, George Benson, Chick Corea, Allan Holdsworth, and Scott Henderson. Each of these jazz stars was unafraid to experiment with his music. Williams responded to their changing sounds, and he especially began to be influenced by Corea. Some critics who listen to Williams now think his style most resembles Corea's.

He developed his artistic technique as well as his ability to express emotions. Musicians need both. His playing led to composing. He first composed tunes in his head, melodies that came and went and came back again. Then he wrote them down. Williams has said to reporters, "I spend a lot of time thinking about music. Not always playing, but thinking about melodies and rhythms. It's something that stays with you for the whole day." Williams began to think about recording some of his compositions, and his fame as a Yankee opened many doors for him.

THE JOURNEY WITHIN

On a very cold day in mid-January 2003, Williams walked into Globe Studios in New York to record his first album. Globe

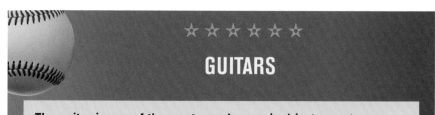

★ ★ ★ ★ ★

GUITARS

The guitar is one of the most popular musical instruments ever invented. Although some form of the guitar has been in existence for hundreds of years, its first golden age was during the nineteenth century. The classical or Spanish guitar came into wide use then. It allowed a performer to throw away the bow traditionally used for a stringed instrument and use his or her fingers to pluck (using the fingernails or fingertips) or strum (using the backs of the fingernails) the six strings of the guitar. The sound of the plucked or strummed string is amplified by the body of the guitar, and the wide variety of sounds the fingers could make astounded early listeners.

Guitars had wood tops often made of spruce, and sides and backs crafted from rosewood, maple, or laminations of many woods. The necks are usually made from mahogany, and the fingerboards from rosewood or ebony. The combinations of woods allowed for different tones in different guitars. All guitars were originally "acoustic" guitars, whether their strings were made of animal intestines, nylon, or steel. The standard six-string versions

Studios is a prestigious recording studio, and many stars (including Sheryl Crow) have recorded hits there. Producer Loren Harriet assembled an all-star cast to accompany Williams as background musicians. Rubén Blades, the Grammy Award-winning singer who has made salsa music a world favorite, was there. So was banjo player Béla Fleck and salsa legend Gilberto Santa Rosa. Bassist Leland Sklar and drummer Kenny Aronoff were also part of this very talented group. Blades knew Williams as the center fielder for the Yankees, and he told a reporter that he thought the group was just going to help Williams fulfill a lead-guitar fantasy. Blades was surprised:

☆ ☆ ☆ ☆ ☆

were varied to include a 12-string guitar made famous by the blues musician Leadbelly and the folk artist Pete Seeger.

The first electric, or non-acoustic, guitars began to appear in the 1930s. By the early 1950s, the Fender Electric Instrument Manufacturing Company was producing the first commercially successful electric guitar, the Telecaster. Leo Fender, who could not play the guitar, designed a newer version he called the Stratocaster, a name intended to make people think of the exciting jet airplanes that were just appearing. It had more complicated electronics than the Telecaster and a sleek design with cutaways for easier access to the neck. Singer Buddy Holly made it famous, and his gravestone in Lubbock, Texas, features a carving of his Stratocaster. Jimi Hendrix and Eric Clapton perfected the Fender twang. The Stratocaster is now the most enduring and famous model of electric guitar in the world. It is still made, although after CBS bought Fender in 1965, musicians soon complained about a lower quality of sound. Stratocasters made in the pre-CBS days have recently sold for more than $75,000.

Famed salsa singer Rubén Blades is pictured here during a May 2002 concert in Panama City in his native Panama. Blades accompanied Bernie Williams on Williams's debut album, *The Journey Within*, and had praise for his work as a musician.

We got in there and he [Williams] was really, really good. . . . I've played with everyone. Salsa, jazz, rock. I've played with a lot of people and listened to a lot of music over 30 years. You recognize quality immediately. . . . What he has done is like jumping in a pool and, on the way down, he's trying to find out if there is any water in it. I think there is a lot of water in there for Bernie.

Eleven songs were recorded, seven of which were composed by Williams. They were assembled into an album titled *The Journey Within,* which was released by GRP Records in July 2003 to rave reviews. The album was treated not as a novelty by a Yankees star but as a serious contribution to modern jazz. "The debut guitar disc from the center fielder for the New York Yankees is no jock vanity project," said a review in the *Philadelphia Inquirer.* "As on the diamond, so in the studio: Williams is a graceful player with speed, as he proves on the first track, 'La Salsa en Mi.' He's also a switch-hitter, equally adept on electric and acoustic." Singer Paul McCartney had become a Yankee fan when he attended his first baseball game in 2001, a World Series game between the Yankees and the Arizona Diamondbacks. When McCartney was given a copy of Williams's CD, he said he "was blown away by his talent." He even signed Williams to a publishing contract (McCartney owns one of the largest musical-publishing firms in the world).

The Journey Within has a smooth jazz sound, but it also reflects Latin roots on such tracks as "La Salsa en Mi" and "Para Don Berna." Williams says he drew on his own life for inspiration:

> Almost all the songs on the CD are from my experiences, things with my wife, my son, and my father, things like that. I think it's a very powerful form for me to express my feelings more than I could express by words. Everyone who knows me knows I don't really talk that much.

"Para Don Berna" is a heartfelt tribute to his father. The song is even more memorable because his brother, Hiram,

plays cello on the track. It is a family affair. Some have compared it to Eric Clapton's "Tears in Heaven"—a tribute by
Clapton to his young son, who died in an accident in 1991.
Williams told a reporter that "I hoped I'd get to play it for my
father. The song helped in my grieving process. It didn't put
closure on my relationship with my father. It put closure on
my grieving."

"Enter the Bond" has a pulsating beat that is more aggressive than the rest of the album, showing the range of Williams's
interests and talents. It is a tribute to James Bond and martial
arts movies, both of which Williams enjoys. "Bernie Jr." is a
quieter track that springs from his love of his son, Bernie: "He
could be a fireball and have this passionate view to life, and at
the same time be such a loving and caring kid." Other pieces
show his humorous side. "Stranded on the Bridge" is based
on an incident when Williams was riding his motorcycle on
a bridge in New York. The motorcycle broke down, so people
honked and yelled obscenities at him as they passed. Since
he had a full face helmet on, no one knew who he was. As he
pushed his motorcycle off the bridge, the clicking of the wheels
over the road made him think of the ticking of a clock, and the
horns in the background added chaos to the monotony of the
ticking. It all became a source of music for Williams, an acci-
dental jazz concert.

"Just Because" is a love letter to Waleska. "In the melody
line, I sort of raise the tone three times, but each time I do it
differently. It's saying, 'Thank you for being who you are. . . .
Thanks, I love you.'" "La Salsa en Mi" is a tribute to his hometown of Vega Alta. The title means "The Salsa in Me," but it also
can be interpreted as "The Salsa in E," since the song is in the
key of E. Cuts from his CD not only included his compositions,
but also covers of Billy Joel's "And So It Goes" and Kansas's
"Dust in the Wind."

Williams was pleased with how his first album sounded.
He felt he had expressed simple but powerful ideas with a nice

melodic line and a few changes of rhythms. The music seemed clear to him. "For me it's a base to expand. From now on, what I come up with will probably be more elaborate."

ONE NIGHT IN CHICAGO

Because Williams was in the middle of the baseball season, only one concert was scheduled to coincide with the release of *The Journey Within*. It was at the House of Blues on North Dearborn Street in Chicago. House of Blues, which is an imposing building, opened in 1996 with a grand ceremony, and its owners included actors Dan Aykroyd and Jim Belushi. It is a music hall, a restaurant/bar, and a hotel. The music hall is modeled after a grand opera house in Prague and can hold more than 1,000 people. House of Blues has featured some of the most famous jazz, blues, and rock artists of the past decade, and on July 13, 2003, it featured Bernie Williams.

Williams had to fly to Chicago directly from Toronto, following a day game with the Blue Jays. His mother, Rufina, was waiting for him in Chicago, as was brother Hiram, Waleska, and all of the Williams children. The concert was a grand event for a family reunion. He knew his father would have been very proud.

Williams told reporter Jack Curry that he was nervous before the 45-minute set, but that "one thing I have going for me is I'm a baseball player playing a guitar. . . . There should be people who are just happy to see me up there playing." People were happy indeed. The happiest of all were his family members.

THE ONCE AND FUTURE MUSICIAN

Williams thinks about what kind of musical career he will have after baseball. He is reluctant to take on the life of a professional guitar player who may have to be on the road and away from his family as often as a professional athlete. He knows his musical skills are still growing and his musical interests are always changing. The attraction of fusing traditional jazz with salsa and other Latin and Brazilian beats is a strong one.

Bernie Williams appeared at the House of Blues in Chicago on July 13, 2003, to promote his album. Earlier in the day, he played in a game in Toronto against the Blue Jays. His whole family attended the concert.

He also knows that the songs in his head are never going away. His technical expertise has developed enough for him to become a professional performer, but composing may become his primary focus after baseball. The McCartney contract is a real start to this next phase of Williams's musical career. The challenges of jazz composition are increasingly complex, and Williams always loves a challenge.

He will have plenty of musical inspirations. He and Waleska are often found looking for new musical clubs in New York. His debut album has meant that he is taken more seriously by young musicians who may want to work with him and learn from him. The pupil will eventually become the teacher. Teaching is a task that comes naturally to him. It is in his blood.

8

A New
Yankee Legend

Center fielders for the New York Yankees play a position that may be the most famous and storied one in sports. Fans of Green Bay Packer quarterbacks (like Bart Starr and Brett Favre), UCLA centers (think of Kareem Abdul-Jabbar and Bill Walton), USC tailbacks, or New York Giant linebackers may disagree about which position has the most storied history, but the list of Yankee center-field greats is a long one.

Earle Combs batted lead-off in front of Babe Ruth and Lou Gehrig from 1924 to 1935, hitting .325 for his career and only retiring after he fractured his skull when he ran into the center-field wall. Joe DiMaggio took over for Combs in 1936 and won a World Championship in each of his first four seasons, the only professional athlete to achieve that. DiMaggio was a three-time Most Valuable Player and appeared in the

Center field has been a storied position for the New York Yankees. Two of the team's most famous center fielders were Joe DiMaggio and Mickey Mantle. Here, the two played alongside each other in a 1951 game (Mantle is at right). That season was DiMaggio's last with the Yankees. Mantle moved from right field to center field the following year.

All-Star Game 13 times. Many baseball experts consider his 56-game hitting streak in 1941 to be the most difficult major-sports performance ever. It is a record that will most likely never be broken. Mickey Mantle took over where DiMaggio left off. Mantle was also a three-time MVP, went to 16 All-Star Games, and won seven World Championships. Every Yankee center fielder after Mantle had a heavy burden to bear. None carried that load as well as Bernie Williams.

Williams's list of on-field accomplishments is a long one. He was a major part of four World Championships for the Yankees. He improved his batting average every year from 1993 to 1999, with one exception in 1996, when he hit only two percentage points lower than in 1995. He is second only to Ken Griffey, Jr., among center fielders over the past 15 years in on-base percentage and slugging percentage. He is among the top 10 Yankees of all time in hits, doubles, home runs, and runs batted in. After the 2006 season, he was in fourth place, just behind Mickey Mantle, for most career hits as a Yankee. He is third in career at-bats, second in doubles, fifth in runs scored, and sixth in home runs for a Yankee. He was the first player ever to hit a home run from both sides of the plate in a postseason game. He received four consecutive Gold Glove awards from 1997 to 2000.

Williams joined the very exclusive club of "100-100" when he scored more than 100 runs and drove in more than 100 runs in five seasons, placing him behind only Lou Gehrig (13 times in the "100-100" club), Babe Ruth (11 times), and Joe DiMaggio (8 times) for the Yankees. Williams was an All-Star five times, from 1997 to 2001, and in his peak years from 1997 to 1999, he was among the leaders in batting average and on-base percentage.

Injuries and age have taken their toll on Williams, but when the Yankees most needed him during their injury-filled 2006 season, he continued to get key hits and kept the Yankees at or near the top in the American League pennant race. In 2006, he was more versatile than ever in how he helped the team. He played center field, right field, designated hitter, pinch hitter, and pinch runner, and his clubhouse presence still soothed the team. The Yankee fans love him now, and he has a special place in their hearts. He is the quiet winner. Even George Steinbrenner finally appreciates him.

DEREK JETER AND BERNIE WILLIAMS

Writers Richard Lederer and Alex Belth call Williams and Derek Jeter "The Odd Couple." Yankee pairings like Ruth and Gehrig or Thurman Munson and Reggie Jackson came naturally to New York fans, but only recently has the "Jeter and Williams" duo become a common term of reference for Yankee excellence. They are very different personalities. Jeter is confident, available to the media, and a sex symbol, and he takes an obvious leadership role. Williams is shy, almost always avoids media interviews, is a family man, and has been a leader in a much more indirect way. Yet their value as players to the success of their team is comparable. They have almost identical batting averages, on-base percentages, and slugging percentages. Williams is actually slightly higher than Jeter in many offensive categories, most notably slugging percentage.

Lederer and Belth write that Williams is not rated as highly as Jeter by most fans because Williams has spread his accomplishments over several areas. He hits doubles and home runs, he draws walks, he runs well, he plays a key defensive position, and he bats from both sides of the plate. In a piece called "The Odd Couple" on the Web site All-Baseball.com, they write:

> Jeter is Spiderman, and Williams is Peter Parker. Jeter is the cool extrovert, and Williams is the thoughtful introvert. Jeter does little things that get noticed while Williams is easy to overlook. . . . Unlike Jeter, Williams never possessed a natural instinct for the game. Long-legged and graceful, Williams was nevertheless awkward on the base paths. His soft, round face, his doe eyes, further create an impression of passivity. But like Tim Duncan in basketball, Williams's looks are deceiving: he is a driven, intense performer. . . . Williams seems to have mastered the game by breaking down each

task, each skill into a lesson. Watching him play the outfield, or up at bat is a pleasure because Williams looks like he's playing a private game, one that is separate from the game at hand.

☆ ☆ ☆ ☆ ☆ ☆
THE NATIONAL BASEBALL HALL OF FAME

One of the best-known museums in the United States is in a small upstate New York town named Cooperstown. It is the National Baseball Hall of Fame and Museum, and some 350,000 visitors walk through its doors every year. They look at the Plaque Gallery, which contains plaques of all of the members of the Hall of Fame; they visit the Grandstand Theater, which has films about baseball; they stroll through the Game, a timeline of baseball events that includes rooms on Babe Ruth, Hank Aaron, women in baseball, the Negro Leagues, and much more. On the third floor, the Autumn Glory section is devoted to postseason baseball. These are just a few of the museum highlights.

The Hall of Fame was formed in 1939 by Steven Carlton Clark, a grandson of the founder of the Singer Sewing Machine Company, to try to bring tourists to Cooperstown. The town had been hurt by Prohibition (the farms in the area grew hops for beer) and the Great Depression. A key part of the marketing of the Hall of Fame was the legend (often disputed) that a Civil War hero named Abner Doubleday started the game of baseball in a cow field outside of town. Major-league baseball teams began to see the value of the museum and started to cooperate by sending bats, balls, uniforms, and other artifacts to be displayed there. Many people assume that Major League Baseball owns and runs the Hall of Fame, but that is not the case—a private company owns and manages the Hall.

The comparison of Williams to Tim Duncan is one that several people have made. Joe Torre compared Williams to tennis player Arthur Ashe. Ashe and Duncan were often given a cushion of privacy by fans, and when Williams leaves a

★ ★ ★ ★ ★

Getting elected to the Hall of Fame is the greatest honor a professional baseball player can receive. No other professional sports hall of fame has the prestige and legendary quality that baseball's does. The election process, however, has been controversial and ever-changing. Currently a player, manager, baseball writer, owner, or builder can be elected to the Hall of Fame by either a 75-percent majority of the senior Baseball Writers Association of America (BBWAA) or by the Veterans Committee, made up of many Hall of Fame members. A major-league player must be retired at least five years before he is put on the ballot, and he needs to have at least 10 years of major-league playing time.

The first five players elected to the Hall of Fame were Ty Cobb, Babe Ruth, Honus Wagner, Christy Mathewson, and Walter Johnson. As of 2006, more than 270 people have been inducted into the Hall, including 225 players, 17 managers, 8 umpires, and 28 builders, executives, and organizers. Two of the most famous non-inductees are Shoeless Joe Jackson and Pete Rose, both of whom have been banned for gambling on baseball games. Fans of both players lobby each year to get them admitted into the Hall.

Baseball fans and other tourists journey from all over the world to Cooperstown, to soak in the colorful history of the game and the town. People walking around Cooperstown on a bright summer day, holding ice cream cones and gazing in store windows on Main Street, look as if they never want to leave.

restaurant with teammates he is never the focus of the gathering fans. He likes it that way. He can get a cab and disappear into the night.

Despite their differences, Jeter and Williams should be paired in Yankee history as the two most important pieces of the championship reign from 1996 to 2000. They both hit when they needed to in crucial games, scored critical runs, drove in others with key hits, and projected a team image of excellence and pride. They may be an odd couple, but many hope their statues will be right next to each other in the Baseball Hall of Fame.

A HALL OF FAMER?

Baseball fans have great debates about who should be in the Baseball Hall of Fame. Many think the honor is about more than statistics, but the majority of outfielders in the Hall of Fame have impressive numbers. Most have either 3,000 hits, 500 home runs, or a career average above .300. Williams will probably not reach any of those milestones, although his career average as of the end of the 2006 season was .297. Using very complicated measures of success, however, baseball experts in statistics, called sabermetricians, have rated Williams among the best center fielders ever.

Baseball experts argue about the top 10 center fielders of all time, but several recently have put Williams in that company. Using several measures of success, the rankings often go as follows, from highest-ranked: Ty Cobb, Willie Mays, Mickey Mantle, Tris Speaker, Joe DiMaggio, Ken Griffey, Jr., Duke Snider, Hack Wilson, Bernie Williams, and Larry Doby. All except Griffey and Williams are in the Hall of Fame, and most expect that when Griffey is eligible (five years after he retires), he will be a first-ballot selection.

When Williams becomes eligible for the Hall of Fame, experts disagree on whether he will be elected. For those who have followed his career closely, however, there is little doubt

Bernie Williams waited in the dugout before batting practice prior to Game 1 of the 2006 American League Division Series against the Detroit Tigers. Many baseball insiders place Williams among the top 10 center fielders of all time.

that if he does not become a Hall of Famer, it will be because he did not seek attention from the media and therefore did not became famous enough. If his greatness is measured by the number of World Championships he helped his team win, there can be no argument about whether Williams is a great baseball player. He is.

A PUBLIC FIGURE

Williams has become enough of a public figure to be seen in various places. In the television series *The West Wing*, fictional president Josiah Bartlett says the center fielder for the Yankees is an accomplished classical guitarist. On *Seinfeld*, Williams appears in an episode with Derek Jeter. He can be seen riding his motorcycle around New York City and Westchester County. Fans now know more about him. He loves sketch art. He wears number 51 because he hopes Puerto Rico will become the fifty-first state of the United States. He is called a "Renaissance Man" more often than any other baseball player.

Williams's stature as a musician will surely grow. He will always have his guitar close by. He will always want his family to be close by as well. He will soon be able to enjoy more free time and fewer hotel rooms. He is a beloved figure to those closest to him, and now to even those further away. He may not want to reveal his feelings except through his music, but the day he leaves Yankee Stadium for the last time he will be swept up in a life's worth of memories on and off the field. When he leaves the Yankees, years of sustained greatness will leave with him. The music may not play for him while he bats for the last time, but he will hear a song in his head.

STATISTICS

BERNIE WILLIAMS
Primary position: Center field (also RF, DH)

Full name: Bernabé Williams Figueroa, Jr.
• Born: September 13, 1968, San Juan,
Puerto Rico • Height: 6'2" •
Weight: 205 lbs. • Team: New York
Yankees (1991–2006)

YEAR	TEAM	G	AB	H	HR	RBI	BA
1991	NYY	85	320	76	3	34	.238
1992	NYY	62	261	73	5	26	.280
1993	NYY	139	567	152	12	68	.268
1994	NYY	108	408	118	12	57	.289
1995	NYY	144	563	173	18	82	.307
1996	NYY	143	551	168	29	102	.305
1997	NYY	129	509	167	21	100	.328
1998	NYY	128	499	169	26	97	.339
1999	NYY	158	591	202	25	115	.342
2000	NYY	141	537	165	30	121	.307
2001	NYY	146	540	166	26	94	.307
2002	NYY	154	612	204	19	102	.333
2003	NYY	119	445	117	15	64	.263
2004	NYY	148	561	147	22	70	.262
2005	NYY	141	485	121	12	64	.249
2006	NYY	131	420	118	12	61	.281
TOTALS		2,076	7,869	2,336	287	1,257	.297

Key: NYY = New York Yankees; G = Games; AB = At-bats; H = Hits; HR = Home runs;
RBI = Runs batted in; BA = Batting average

CHRONOLOGY

1968 September 13 Is born Bernabé Williams Figueroa, Jr., in San Juan, Puerto Rico.

1970 Family moves to Vega Alta, Puerto Rico.

1976 Begins to play the Spanish guitar.

1980 Enters the Escuela Libre de Musica, the Free School of Music, a prestigious academy in San Juan for the musically gifted.

1983 Wins four gold medals at an international track meet in San Juan and sets the Puerto Rican record for his age group in the 400-meter dash.

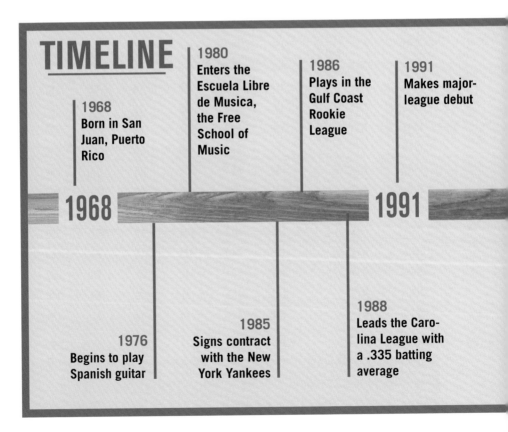

TIMELINE

1968 Born in San Juan, Puerto Rico

1980 Enters the Escuela Libre de Musica, the Free School of Music

1986 Plays in the Gulf Coast Rookie League

1991 Makes major-league debut

1968

1991

1976 Begins to play Spanish guitar

1985 Signs contract with the New York Yankees

1988 Leads the Carolina League with a .335 batting average

1985   Enrolls at the University of Puerto Rico, concentrating in biological science.

September 13   On his seventeenth birthday, signs a professional baseball contract with the New York Yankees.

1986   Plays in the Gulf Coast Rookie League in Fort Lauderdale, Florida.

1987   Becomes a switch-hitter during minor-league spring training.

1988   Plays for the Prince William Cannons in the Carolina League; hits .335, best in the league.

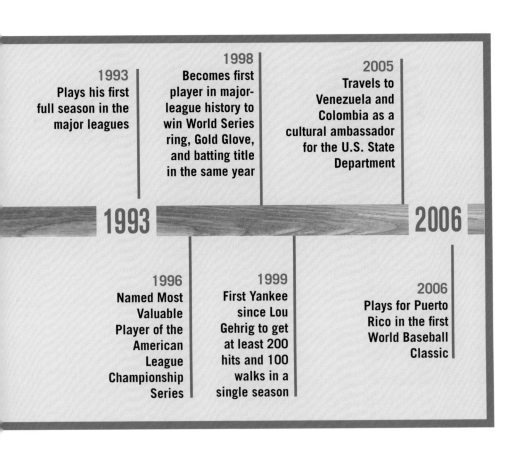

1993
Plays his first full season in the major leagues

1998
Becomes first player in major-league history to win World Series ring, Gold Glove, and batting title in the same year

2005
Travels to Venezuela and Colombia as a cultural ambassador for the U.S. State Department

1993   2006

1996
Named Most Valuable Player of the American League Championship Series

1999
First Yankee since Lou Gehrig to get at least 200 hits and 100 walks in a single season

2006
Plays for Puerto Rico in the first World Baseball Classic

1988   **November** Is added to the Yankees' 40-man roster.

1989   Plays for the Columbus Clippers, the Yankees' Triple-A team; is demoted after 50 games to the Double-A team in Albany, New York.

1990   **February 23** Marries wife, Waleska, in Puerto Rico; son Bernie Alexander is born late in the year.

1991   **July 7** Makes major-league debut against the Baltimore Orioles; has his first RBI with a sacrifice fly to left field.

1992   Plays for Columbus Clippers again; plays 62 games with the Yankees.

1993   Plays his first full season in the major leagues; bats .268, with 12 home runs and 68 runs batted in.

1994   **April 4** Second child, Beatriz Noemi, is born.

1995   **September 14** Third child, Bianca, is born. Has his best season to date, hitting .307, with 18 home runs and 82 runs batted in.

1996   Is named Most Valuable Player of the American League Championship Series after hitting .474; Yankees win World Series.

       November 12 Makes professional musical debut at the Bottom Line in New York City.

1998   Yankees win a record 125 games, including the World Series; Williams wins American League batting title, hitting .339, and also wins Gold Glove, becoming the first player in major-league history to win World Series ring, Gold Glove, and batting title in the same year.

       November 25 Signs his only long-term Yankee contract, seven years for $87.5 million.

1999   Family moves to Armonk, New York; bats .342 for the year, third-highest in league; is the first Yankee since Lou Gehrig to get at least 200 hits and 100 walks in a single season; Yankees win World Series again.

2000   Yankees win third World Series in a row.

2001   Father Bernabé, Sr., dies; Yankees lose a classic World Series to the Arizona Diamondbacks in seven games.

2002   Yankees lose to Anaheim Angels in the American League Division Series.

2003   Undergoes major knee surgery and misses 40 games; Yankees lose World Series to Florida Marlins.

2004   Yankees lose a classic American League Championship Series to the Boston Red Sox in seven games.

2005   Travels to Venezuela and Colombia as a cultural ambassador for the U.S. State Department; becomes a part-time player.

2006   Plays for Puerto Rico in the first World Baseball Classic; after injuries to several Yankee outfielders during the season, fills in and helps team win.

June Plays in 2,000th game.

GLOSSARY

at-bat (AB)   An official turn at batting that is charged to a baseball player, except when the player walks, sacrifices, is hit by a pitched ball, or is interfered with by a catcher. At-bats are used to calculate a player's batting average and slugging percentage.

base on balls   When a batter receives four pitches out of the strike zone, the batter receives a base on balls, also called a walk, and is awarded to first base.

batter's box   The area to the left and right of home plate in which the batter must stand for fair play to take place.

batting average   The number of hits a batter gets divided by the number of times the player is at bat. For example, 3 hits in 10 at-bats would be a .300 batting average.

bullpen   The area where pitchers warm up, usually behind the outfield fences. The name comes from its similarity to where bulls are kept before a bullfight.

catcher   The defensive player directly behind home plate. The player's job is to signal to the pitcher which kind of pitch to throw and where to throw it, and then catch the pitch. Good catchers know hitters' strengths and weaknesses and can "frame" their catches to influence umpires to call more strikes.

designated hitter   In the American League, a player who bats each time for the pitcher. There is no designated hitter in the National League. Baseball is the only professional sport in which different rules apply in different sections of the league. The lack of consistency about the designated hitter is an ongoing debate.

double play   A play by the defense during which two offensive players are put out in a continuous action.

dugout   The area where the players and managers not on the field can wait and watch. It usually has a bench with a roof, and in the major leagues includes a bat rack, glove and towel holders, a water cooler, a telephone to the bullpen, and more.

earned-run average (ERA)   The average number of runs a pitcher allows per nine-inning game; the runs must be scored without errors by defensive players.

error   The game's scorer designates an error when a defensive player makes a mistake that results in a runner reaching base or advancing.

fair ball   A ball hit between the two foul lines that run down first base and third base to the stands and beyond. Fair territory is the part of the playing field between the first- and third-base foul lines, extending into the stands and beyond. The foul lines themselves are in fair territory.

fastball   A pitch that is thrown more for high velocity than for movement; it is the most common type of pitch.

fielding percentage   A statistic that reflects the percentage of times a defensive player successfully handles a batted or thrown ball. It is calculated by the sum of putouts and assists divided by the number of total chances.

foul ball   A batted ball that lands in foul territory, which is the part of the playing field that is outside the first- and third-base foul lines. The foul lines themselves are in fair territory.

grand slam   A home run with three runners on base, resulting in four runs for the offensive team. The grand slam is one of the most dramatic plays in baseball.

home run   When a batter hits a ball into the stands in fair territory, it is a home run. The batter may also have an inside-the-park home run if the ball never leaves the play-ing field and the runner is able to reach home plate without stopping before being tagged by a defensive player. A home run counts as one run, and if there are any runners on base when a home run is hit, they too score.

inning   The time during which both teams have come to bat and each has made three outs. The top of an inning is when the visiting team comes to bat, and the bottom of an inning is when the home team comes to bat. In professional base-ball, a standard game is nine innings. In college baseball, it may be seven or nine. In Little League, it may be three to six innings.

knuckleball   A pitch thrown without spin—traditionally thrown with the knuckles, but also with the fingertips. It generally flutters and moves suddenly on its way to the plate.

line drive   A batted ball, usually hit hard, that never gets too far off the ground. Typically a line drive will get beyond the infield without touching the ground, or will be hit directly at a player and be caught before it touches the ground.

on-base percentage (OBP)   The number of times a player reaches base divided by the number of plate appearances.

perfect game   A very rare no-hitter during which each batter is consecutively retired, allowing no baserunners via walks, errors, or other means.

runs batted in (RBI)   The number of runs that score as a direct result of a batter's hit(s) are the runs batted in by that batter. The major-league record is 191 RBIs for a single year by one batter.

sabermetrics   The study of baseball using nontraditional statistics. Traditional baseball performance measurement focuses on batting average, hits, home runs, and earned-run average. Sabermetrics tries to measure those statistics that predict winning and losing most accurately. On-base percentage and slugging percentage are two key sabermetric statistics.

slugging percentage (SLG) The number of bases a player reaches divided by the number of at-bats. It is a measure of the power of a batter.

strike zone The area directly over home plate up to the batter's chest (roughly where the batter's uniform lettering is) and down to his or her knees. Different umpires have slightly different strike zones, and players only ask that they be consistent.

switch-hitter A player who can hit from both sides of the plate.

umpire The official who rules on plays. For most baseball games, a home-plate umpire calls balls and strikes, and another umpire in the infield rules on outs at bases.

walk-off home run A game-ending home run by the home team—so named because the losing team has to walk off the field.

World Series A championship series, usually the best four out of seven games. In Major League Baseball, the World Series comes after teams have been through a League Division Series (a best three-out-of-five series) and a League Championship Series (a best four-out-of-seven series).

BIBLIOGRAPHY

Adair, Robert K. *The Physics of Baseball.* 3rd ed. New York: HarperCollins, 2002.

Berkow, Ira. "This Bernie Is Not Some Banjo Hitter." *New York Times*, November 12, 1996.

Bondy, Filip. "Another in Columbus Crew Gets to Discover Stadium." *New York Times*, July 8, 1991.

Curry, Jack. "It's Not the Bronx, but Williams Feels at Home." *New York Times*, March 8, 2006.

———. "Plucking at a Star's Heartstrings." *New York Times*, February 18, 2005.

———. "Upon Further Review, Williams Can Still Deliver." *New York Times*, October 5, 2003.

———. "Williams's Father Dies of a Heart Attack." *New York Times*, May 15, 2001.

———. "Williams's Long Run with the Yankees Winds Down." *New York Times*, June 15, 2005.

Deveney, Sean. "Forging a Special Bond." *Sporting News*, December 13, 1999.

Haudricourt, Tom. "Swing and a Hit Bernie Williams." *The Record* (Bergen County, New Jersey), March 13, 2003.

Kepner, Tyler. "Soaking Up New Role and Another Spring as a Yankee." *New York Times*, February 28, 2006.

Ladson, William. "The '98 Yankees: The Greatest Season, but Not the Greatest Team." *Sporting News*, November 2, 1998.

Lederer, Richard, and Alex Belth. "The Odd Couple." *Bronx Banter.* February 25, 2004. Available online at *http://www.all-baseball.com/bronxbanter/archives/012058.html.*

Lewis, Michael. *Moneyball: The Art of Winning an Unfair Game.* New York: W.W. Norton, 2003.

Martinez, Michael. "Spring Phenom a Yankee Perennial." *New York Times*, February 26, 1989.

Olney, Buster. "Highest-Paid Yankee Still Walks Alone." *New York Times,* July 15, 1999.

———. "Williams's Production Is Worth the Wait." *New York Times,* March 18, 2001.

———. "Williams Puts Value in Hard Work." *New York Times,* July 4, 2000.

Rhoden, William C. "Bernie Williams Back Home and Keeping the Faith." *Puerto Rico Herald,* April 21, 2001.

Smith, Claire. "Bernie Williams: From Bambi to Tiger." *New York Times,* September 21, 1995.

———. "Portrait of the Artist as a Center Fielder." *New York Times,* November 7, 1994.

———. "Speak Softly, Run Swiftly, Swing Powerfully." *New York Times,* October 18, 1996.

FURTHER READING

BOOKS

Harper, John, and Bob Klapisch. *Champions!* New York: Villard Books, 1996.

Kernan, Kevin. *Bernie Williams: Quiet Superstar.* Champaign, Ill.: Sports Publishing, 1999.

King, George. *Unbeatable! The Historic Season of the 1998 World Champion New York Yankees.* New York: HarperCollins, 1998.

Stout, Glenn. *Yankees Century: 100 Years of New York Yankees Baseball.* Boston: Houghton Mifflin, 2002.

Vancil, Mark, and Mark Mandrake. *The Greatest Yankees Teams.* New York: Ballantine Books, 2004.

WEB SITES

Baseball Almanac
http://www.baseball-almanac.com

Baseball Reference
http://www.baseball-reference.com

BW: Bernie Williams
http://www.berniewilliams.com

Bernie Williams Fan Tribute Page
http://www.berniewilliams.net

MLB.com
http://mlb.mlb.com/index.jsp

National Baseball Hall of Fame
http://www.baseballhalloffame.org

New York Yankees
http://newyork.yankees.mlb.com

PICTURE CREDITS

INDEX

ABOUT THE AUTHOR

CLIFFORD W. MILLS is a writer and editor living in Jacksonville, Florida. He has written biographies of Derek Jeter, Pope Benedict XVI, and Virginia Woolf, compiled a volume of essays about J.D. Salinger, and has worked as an editor for John Wiley and Sons and Oxford University Press. He played baseball in college and had dreams of playing third base for the Yankees.